The Battle of Megiddo, Palestine 1918

Combined Arms and the Last Great Cavalry Charge

Eric W. Osborne

 Helion & Company

Helion & Company Limited
Unit 8 Amherst Business Centre
Budbrooke Road
Warwick
CV34 5WE
England
Tel. 01926 499 619
Email: info@helion.co.uk
Website: www.helion.co.uk
Twitter: @helionbooks
Visit our blog at blog.helion.co.uk

Published by Helion & Company 2023
Designed and typeset by Mach 3 Solutions (www.mach3solutions.co.uk)
Cover designed by Paul Hewitt, Battlefield Design (www.battlefield-design.co.uk)

Text © Eric W. Osborne 2023
Maps drawn by Nat Case, INCase, LLC, Relief imagery ESRI © Eric W. Osborne 2023
Cover © Imperial War Museum Q12386 Gloucestershire Yeomanry passing through Damascus, 2 October 1918.

Every reasonable effort has been made to trace copyright holders and to obtain their permission for the use of copyright material. The author and publisher apologize for any errors or omissions in this work and would be grateful if notified of any corrections that should be incorporated in future reprints or editions of this book.

ISBN 9-7-81804513-29-3

British Library Cataloguing-in-Publication Data.
A catalogue record for this book is available from the British Library.

All rights reserved. No part of this publication may be reproduced, stored in a retrieval system, or transmitted, in any form, or by any means, electronic, mechanical, photocopying, recording or otherwise, without the express written consent of Helion & Company Limited.

For details of other military history titles published by Helion & Company Limited contact the above address or visit our website: http://www.helion.co.uk.

We always welcome receipt of book proposals from prospective authors.

Contents

Acknowledgements	iv
Introduction: Importance of the Battle of Megiddo	v
1 Pre-War Europe and the Ottoman Empire before the Outbreak of War	11
2 Allied Shift from the Defense of Egypt to Offensives into Palestine Strategic and Political Motivations	28
3 Planning and Preparations	53
4 Battle	66
5 Military and Political Ramifications	92
Bibliography	109
Index	117

Acknowledgements

This book would not have been possible without the help and support of a host of people. I would like to thank Dr Rose Mary Sheldon for her professional guidance and support as my colleague, friend, and greatly accomplished historian. I would also like to thank the kind and professional staff of the National Archives of the United Kingdom, Imperial War Museum, Liddell Hart Centre for Military Archives, King's College, London and the interlibrary loan staff of Virginia Military Institute. Without the help of these individuals this volume would not have been possible. I would also like to express my admiration for Helion & Company Ltd and specifically my editor Dr Michael LoCicero. It has been a pleasure to work with such a fine publisher.

I would also like to thank my wife, Kim, as I could not possibly have done this work without her support. Finally, I would like to thank my parents, Dr Larry Osborne and Mrs. Susan Osborne, my brother Jack E. Osborne and his wife Shera, as well as my children Jordan, Madi, and Ian.

Introduction: Importance of the Battle of Megiddo

Studies on a myriad of military, diplomatic, and social aspects of First World War abound as a result of the centennial of the Great War in 2014. The focus of a great deal of these works remains the Western Front in keeping with the prevalent idea that it was the most crucial theater of the war as opposed to others such as the Eastern Front or Middle Eastern Front. Nonetheless, an increasing amount of scholarly attention is being paid to other, lesser appreciated areas of the world within the context of the Great War. One of these is the Middle East, where primarily British forces faced those of the Ottoman Empire. Assessments of events in this area during First World War are vital to an understanding of the state of this region in the modern world since British success against the Ottomans contributed to the collapse of the empire and a restructuring of the Middle East that would continue to pose the threat of an unstable world from the outset in areas such as Palestine and Syria.

A key event for understanding how the Middle East transitioned from 400 years of Ottoman rule towards its current state is the Battle of Megiddo, being an operation that unfolded between 19-21 September 1918 that devastated the Ottoman Army. It also allowed for a series of drives that subsequently left the British in control of all of present-day Palestine, Syria, Lebanon, and a rather small portion of southern Turkey.

Its ramifications for the world were certainly not evident at the time of the battle. Indeed, the Battle of Megiddo unfolded in a theater of operations that largely languished for much of the war as the Allies focused the majority of their attention on the Western Front. In the wake of the Ottoman declaration of war against the Allies in November 1914, Allied goals in the Middle East rested on three objectives: the seizure of Mesopotamian oil fields, the opening of the Dardanelles Straits in order to supply Russia, and the defense of the Suez Canal in Egypt as a vital link for Britain to the supplies afforded by its eastern empire. British forces bore the brunt of the operations to accomplish these goals since they had controlled Egypt for decades because of their need to defend the Suez Canal. By the end of 1915 the Allies had achieved only limited success in pursuit of these objectives. Operations in Mesopotamia resulted in early successes through the capture of Basra on 22 November 1914 and the conquest of Qurna on 9 December while efforts to expand the defensive perimeter for these areas through attacks up the Tigris and Euphrates towards Baghdad resulted in a defeat at the 22-26 November 1915 Battle of Ctesiphon and a British withdrawal to Kut-al-Amara, where British forces became besieged by those of the Ottomans. While this setback occurred, the Allies suffered disaster between March and December 1915 in their attempts to open the Dardanelles Straits. Only in the defense of Egypt did the British enjoy definitive success as their forces repulsed an Ottoman attack on the Suez Canal in February 1915. None of these operations entailed any potential seizure of Ottoman territory in the Near East past coastal regions around the Dardanelles.

Only in 1916 did the British undertake operations aimed at conquering large portions of Ottoman territory in the Near East and these unfolded solely in keeping with the goal of effectively defending the Suez Canal. In early 1916 General Sir Archibald Murray, the newly appointed commander of the Egyptian Expeditionary Force based in Egypt, sought to protect the Suez Canal through an active defense that required the conquest of the Sinai Peninsula. Murray accomplished this goal by the end of the year, but he did so in an atmosphere where the Egyptian Expeditionary Force became increasingly smaller as a reflection of the Near East continuing to be a theater of secondary importance to the Allies versus the Western Front. General Sir William Robertson, Chief of the British Imperial General Staff, progressively diverted the forces of the Egyptian Expeditionary Force to France for operations against Germany. Robertson, like many others in the Allied High Command, was a "Westerner," believing that the war could only be won on the Western Front and consequently it had top priority in terms of manpower commitment.

This situation only began to change after December 1916 with the accession of David Lloyd George as Prime Minister of Great Britain. Unlike many in the political and military hierarchy of the Allies, he was an "Easterner" in terms of his strategic outlook on the war. Lloyd George looked to winning the war against Germany through a peripheral strategy directed at Germany's allies, particularly the Ottoman Empire. This approach entailed a drive by the British Expeditionary Force into southern Palestine with Jerusalem as the objective. Murray's limited success led to his replacement in June 1917 by General Sir Edmund Allenby who managed, by 9 December 1917, to conquer southern Palestine and take Jerusalem. Allenby's plans for further operations in keeping with Lloyd George's vision were, however, disrupted by the siphoning off of the lion's share of his experienced troops to the Western Front to stem the massive Ludendorff Offensive of Spring 1918. The result was a period between March and late September 1918 that saw few offensive operations by the Egyptian Expeditionary Force as Allenby received imperial troops, mostly Indians, in place of those soldiers dispatched to the Western Front and endeavored to train them and rebuild his army.

The Battle of Megiddo (19-21 September 1918) represents the return of the Egyptian Expeditionary Force to the offensive. By this time, Allenby's army occupied a position along a line between Jericho and Jaffa with a force that far outnumbered the Turks. Allenby commanded a force of 57,000 infantry and 11,000 cavalry with 552 guns. Supplementing this force was a 30,000-man Arab army of irregular cavalry commanded by Emir Feisal with Major T.E. Lawrence acting as liaison to Allenby. This force was the product of the Arab uprising of 1916 fomented by the British to de-stabilize the Ottoman Empire in return for the promise of a pan-Arab state at the end of the war.

The Ottoman Yildirim Army Group, commanded by German General Liman von Sanders, on the other hand could muster only 32,000 infantry, 3,000 cavalry, and 370 pieces of artillery against the Allied troops. Sanders arrayed his forces in three armies spanning the region of Es Salt in the Jordan Valley to the Mediterranean. Not only were the Ottomans outnumbered, but the troops, unlike their British counterparts, were undersupplied and generally demoralized. Both of these problems were the result of two factors that plagued the Ottomans throughout the war: the first and more fundamental problem was that the Ottomans lacked the manpower and resources to fight on multiple fronts effectively. Added to this problem was the decision of Minister of War Enver Pasha to concentrate the majority of the resources that he had on the Caucasus Front by late 1918 following the Bolshevik Revolution of Russia that toppled the government and forced the country out of the war. Enver justified the diversion of troops and supplies in the name of using the chaos that the revolution created to effectively seize territory in the Caucasus area. This decision exacerbated the problems of manpower and supply and proved mortal ones to the Ottoman defense of Palestine.

Allenby, being a cavalryman by training, envisioned an operation to destroy the three armies of the Yildirim Army Group through the use of cavalry as the main striking force. He plan called for penetrating Turkish defenses near the coast through a short artillery barrage followed by an infantry attack. Once Turkish lines were breached, cavalry units would pour through and envelop the Turkish armies by cutting off their communications and their avenues of escape north. Unlike the Western Front, the use of cavalry was a viable option given the terrain of Palestine near the coast in the Plain of Sharron, and the fact that the Ottoman defensive lines were not as deep as those on the Western Front and were thus easier to breach quickly. In conjunction with the striking force of cavalry, Allenby also planned to use aircraft to attack Ottoman forces as they attempted to retreat.

Allenby depended on surprise and mass attack for success. He consequently used his air superiority over the Ottomans to mask his troop movements while at the same time setting up an elaborate deception in the form of false fortifications and a command headquarters in the Jordan Valley area of the front to convince the Ottomans that the offensive would take place there.

By the opening of the battle on 19 September 1918, Allenby had concentrated three quarters of his force near the coastal area of Palestine that would be the true site of the assault against the Ottomans. Following a fifteen minute artillery barrage, the infantry of the Egyptian Expeditionary Force overwhelmed Ottoman defensive positions allowing for the charge of the cavalry in what became the last great cavalry engagement of history. By the end of 21 September, Allenby's plan had proved a stunning success with the destruction of two Ottoman armies and the decimation of the third while the Egyptian Expeditionary Force suffered less than 1,000 dead. Ottoman losses and consequently weakness allowed Allenby to launch further operations over the course of October that resulted in the conquest of all of Palestine, Syria, and Lebanon before the Turkish call for an armistice on 30 October 1918 to negotiate peace.

The Battle of Megiddo resulted in great loss for the Ottomans in terms of both men and material. It ranks as one of the most successful operations of the entire war for the Allies or the Central Powers. Even so, few works cover the battle in depth. The most recent work, Bryan Perrett's *Megiddo 1918: Lawrence, Allenby, and the March on Damascus*, published first in 1999 and reprinted in 2004, gives an effective general overview of the contest, but is more of a popular work rather than a scholarly one. There is little coverage of the strategic context of the battle or its ramifications for the war and the Middle East in the postwar era. Additionally, the work lacks a bibliography and relies on only eleven secondary sources cited in a section on additional readings concerning the battle. The other work most commonly consulted that deals solely with Megiddo is Cyril Fall's *Armageddon 1918* published in 1964. Falls was one of Britain's official historians who wrote works on the history of Britain in the war. While it is a good operational account, he relies heavily on his 1930 work, *The History of the Great War – Military Operations Egypt and Palestine* while supplementing it with an additional 19 sources. As it relies on Britain's official history of the war, this volume contains precious little about the Ottoman forces that opposed the Egyptian Expeditionary Force. Additionally, it provides scant information concerning British preparations for the battle and contains no citations to reference sources.

The majority of writing about the Battle of Megiddo is contained in books devoted to wider subjects of the war, histories and memoirs of those that served in the Palestinian and Syrian theater, and unit histories. The first of these categories contain good works, but not ones that provide much in-depth examination due to their scope. An example is David Woodward's *Hell in the Holy Land: First World War in the Middle East*. Published in 2006, the Battle of Megiddo appears on only sixteen of its 233 pages. More detailed examinations exist in Edward Erickson's works concerning the Ottoman Army in First World War, but the focus on the performance of the army in the war does not allow for a great deal of coverage of the Battle of Megiddo itself. More detailed examinations of Megiddo exist in works concerning General Edmund Allenby as the commander of the Egyptian Expeditionary Force. By far the best work on Allenby is that of Matthew Hughes with his *Allenby and British Strategy in the Middle East* published in 1999. The author places Megiddo within the context of overall British strategy in the region, but even so the battle still does not garner a great deal of coverage as a focus on the conflict is not the author's aim. Earlier works concerning Allenby also cover Megiddo, such as Archibald Wavell's, *Allenby: A Study in Greatness* published in 1941, but it illustrates the fact that many who wrote on Allenby were those who had served with him in the Middle East. As a result, they do not examine Allenby or the Battle of Megiddo in a critical light. Wavell also published a work on the Palestine campaigns that exhibited the same lack of critical analysis concerning Allenby. Memoirs abound from individuals that served under Allenby's command. While certainly helpful in providing the personal side of events that unfolded during the Battle of Megiddo, these cannot stand alone as authoritative studies due to events being portrayed solely through the experience of one person and thus author bias. Finally, the Battle of Megiddo finds its place in a host of histories concerning units or branches of the military that served in the contest. These are helpful for understanding the actions of a portion of the Egyptian Expeditionary Force, but like memoirs they are a bit myopic in scope.

This volume seeks to provide a detailed, scholarly coverage of the Battle of Megiddo as one of the most successful military engagements of First World War and one that showcases not only its importance militarily, but also its effects on the British Empire and world in the postwar era. In military terms I have placed greater emphasis on the role played by logistics both by the Egyptian Expeditionary Force and the Ottomans. While General Allenby had force in greater numbers, the Battle of Megiddo was won and lost through good logistics for the British and poor logistics for the Ottomans. It will also provide greater coverage of the importance of the infantry and air force in deciding the contest. Most works on Megiddo to date portray it as a battle won by cavalry. While the cavalry certainly played the critical role, its success would have been impossible without the work of the infantry that breached enemy defenses and pushed Ottoman forces north through Palestine into the British cavalry that lay in wait in the Ottoman rear. Far more emphasis must also be paid to the Royal Air Force and its critical role in the outcome of the Battle of Megiddo. The contest would not have unfolded as it did without the meticulous reconnaissance work carried out by the air force before the battle and the crippling attacks it mounted on Ottoman communications systems and retreating forces. Finally, this work seeks to correct a common problem in many books that attribute the success at Megiddo to the brilliance of General Allenby. While he was certainly a fine leader, the outcome of Megiddo was not due to any strategic or tactical genius that he possessed but was the result of his fine corps commanders and staff. He also owes his success in large part to the diminished capacity of the Ottoman Army by late 1918.

This work will treat Megiddo as not only a militarily significant event, but also one that played a part in British imperial history. By October 1918, the vast majority of the Egyptian Expeditionary Force comprised Indian troops rather than European; many of these were Muslim. The incorporation of Indians into Allenby's army is a fine illustration of the role played by the British Empire in the war and the perceived difficulties attendant with the use of Indians in battle in Palestine and Syria. Training posed a challenge since many were not ready for combat and as a result European soldiers questioned their potential worth. There was also a concern about the political consequences of deploying Muslim Indian troops in an area held sacred by Islam. The British India Office, that presided over India, believed that since the majority of Muslim Indians were pro-Turkish their use in battle against the Ottomans might lead to civil unrest back in India which might undermine imperial control. In retrospect, this military concern proved entirely unfounded, and this work will provide coverage to Indians in the Battle of Megiddo since prior works do not greatly emphasize their importance. The Battle of Megiddo showed the value of the Indian soldier. Indeed, most of the contest for the British was fought primarily by Indians. On the other hand, political concerns over the use of Indians did carry some weight. Indian nationalists, particularly Muslim Indians, began to call for a greater degree of self-rule in

India as a result of their participation in First World War, and held up the sacrifice of Indians in Palestine and Syria as justification. Muslim Indian nationalists saw the British commitment to a pan-Arab state and their support of a Zionist state in these regions and called for the same treatment in keeping with President Woodrow Wilson's Fourteen Points that championed the self-determination of peoples. While the agitation of Muslim Indian nationalists did not lead to a revolt throughout the sub-continent of India, it certainly did fuel the political discussion of Indian self-rule in the post-war years.

Finally, this book will highlight the immediate ramifications of Megiddo on the Middle East in order to highlight that this battle, unlike most others, left an indelible mark far after its end. Allenby's success led to a situation upon the close of hostilities with the Ottomans whereby the British presided over all of Palestine, Syria, and Lebanon. The general was a military governor who administered a political power vacuum made greatly unstable by a series of conflicting territorial claims fashioned during the war between Britain and its allies, most notably France and the Arabs. The great success at Megiddo placed the British in this position just as the Egyptian Expeditionary Force was conquering regions in Palestine and Syria where the French and Arabs were trying to assert their claims. The British added to this instability because their crushing success in the Battle of Megiddo led to their trying to repudiate their imperial agreements with France. The British wanted to dominate all land claimed by France for the sake of the British Empire since French forces were virtually non-existent in the Middle Eastern Theater. Finally, through their control of Palestine the British found themselves embroiled in an attempt to found a Zionist state which they had promised to the Jewish community during the war. This was an endeavor that Allenby himself thought would lead to chaos in the region. The political debates over the Middle East that unfolded during the 1919 Paris Peace Conference were merely continuations of debates that began immediately as a consequence of the Battle of Megiddo.

In sum, a new work on the Battle of Megiddo seems timely in this period of renewed emphasis on First World War. Not only do previously covered aspects of the battle require re-assessment, but there is also a need to include a greater examination of some topics that were up to now underemphasized. Finally, a new work on Megiddo that illustrates the effect of the battle on events other than military ones will showcase how this battle's impact transcended the war itself. Megiddo, like First World War in general, permanently altered the world.

1

Pre-War Europe and the Ottoman Empire before the Outbreak of War

The Battle of Megiddo was the culmination of a series of Allied operations against the Ottoman Empire during the First World War. This battle and those before it in Palestine, Syria, Lebanon, and Mesopotamia, showcased the great importance attached by the Entente powers to the defeat of the Ottoman Empire by late 1918. The British, whose forces were primarily involved in the war against the Ottomans, believed that the defeat of the empire would lead to the end of the war overall with the coming to power in 1916 of David Lloyd George as British prime minister. They also had clearly imperial goals for the region in the post-war world in keeping with agreements signed with France and Russia. This emphasis on the defeat of the Ottomans had not been the overriding one at the outset of the war. Indeed, before the outbreak of the war the pursuit of imperial expansion at the expense of the Ottoman Empire was not a goal either. The Battle of Megiddo, however, contributed both to the defeat of the empire and the imperial conquest of the Near East with vast ramifications in the post-war world.

The years spanning the late nineteenth century to the dawn of the First World War were a period that represented the height of British imperial power in a world where virtually none of London's territorial holdings lay in the Near East. At the turn of the twentieth century Great Britain, despite gains being made by Germany and the United States beginning in the late nineteenth century, was the world's leading economic power. The country owed this status in part to its industrial might, which rested chiefly on its empire. Great Britain received raw materials from an empire that in 1914 spanned fully a quarter of the world's landmass with a population of 425 million people. Of these subjects 366 million were non-Caucasian with 316 million of them being Indian.[1] The nation's factories subsequently turned raw materials garnered from the empire into goods for export to both its imperial possessions and the rest of the world. By 1880, Britain accounted for 26 percent of the world's industry and was

---

1   Lawrence James, *The Rise and Fall of the British Empire* (New York: St. Martin's, 1997), 353.

the greatest producer of pig-iron, coal, and steel.[2] In addition to its economic might was the fact that Britain was the leading commercial carrier in the world. In 1894, the value of the carrying trade for Britain exceeded £1,000,000,000, which was a colossal sum in that era. By 1913, the country's maritime fleet totaled 18,696,000 tons of the world's shipping total of 46,970,000 tons.[3]

Despite its vast imperial interests that underpinned its world power, Great Britain throughout the nineteenth century and into the first years of the twentieth showed very little interest in controlling or influencing events in the Ottoman Empire. The exception was Mesopotamia in the early years of the twentieth century. Indeed, British policy throughout the nineteenth century focused primarily on making sure no other imperial power exerted too much influence within Syria, being designated in the years prior to the First World War as the region that encompassed modern-day Syria, Lebanon, Palestine, and the Trans-Jordan. Such a situation could threaten British interests in Egypt, which was informally controlled as part of the empire by the late nineteenth century, and the Suez Canal that represented the shipping lifeline between Britain and its eastern empire, primarily India.[4] Their foreign policy goal meant maintaining the Ottoman Empire in order to protect both Egypt and the Suez Canal. The canal was a facility characterized by Sir Henry Wilson, Chief of the Imperial General Staff in 1918, as the Clapham Junction of Imperial Communications. This was certainly a fair assessment given that the journey from Britain through the Suez Canal to India took some 40 days while a journey from Britain to India around the Cape of Good Hope could take over five months. In addition to the protection of the canal, the British also endeavored to make sure that no imperial power affected their dominance of the Mediterranean Sea. Any loss of Ottoman territory in the region of the eastern Mediterranean could potentially lead to the construction of a naval base by a foreign power that could pose a threat to both these interests.

The two imperial powers that potentially represented challenges for the British in the region of the Near East during the years leading to the First World War were France and Germany. Russia, an additional imperial force, posed a negligible problem to British interests as the main goal of St. Petersburg was to prevent the Dardanelles Straits from falling into the hands of a third power. Russia's interests in other areas of the Ottoman Empire were rather low. While the French and Germans were imperial competitors of Great Britain, their governments shared a common desire with Britain in the last years before the war. None of them wanted a partition of the

---

2   Jon Sumida, *In Defense of Naval Supremacy: Finance, Technology, and British Naval Policy, 1889-1914* (Boston, MA: Unwin Hyman, 1989), 6.
3   E.J. Hobsbawm, *The Age of Empire, 1875-1914* (New York: Vintage Books, 1989), 350. For shipping totals see G.S. Clarke and J.R. Thursfield, *The Navy and the Nation* (London, 1897), 94.
4   Eyal Zisser, "Britain and the Levant, 1918-1946: A Missed Opportunity?" in *Britain and the Middle East: From Imperial Power to Junior Partner*, ed. Zach Levy and Elie Podeh (Portland, OR: Sussex Academic Press, 2008), 136.

Ottoman Empire as it ran counter to their business interests. With respect to France and Germany, the French were certainly the larger consideration for the British in the Near East because they held great influence within Syria as they had for some time prior to the First World War. Even so, the British did not view the French in Syria as much of a threat to their interests since their presence in the region had been long established and recognized by London.[5] French involvement in Syria dated back to 1535 with the Capitulations Treaty between France and the Ottoman Empire. This agreement gave trading privileges to French merchants within the empire. By the eve of the First World War, France was so heavily invested economically in Syria that it held 63 percent of the entire Ottoman public debt. Not only did France have this holding, but in part as a result of it they also controlled most of the operations of the Ottoman Imperial Bank by the late 1890s.[6] The French were the leading investors in both Anatolia and Syria with a monopoly in railroad lines in these areas, although German competition beginning in the late nineteenth century mounted as Germany was the principal financial backer of the Berlin to Baghdad Railroad. France also held substantial interests in ports, gas and electric plants, and silk plants.[7]

As a result of these interests, French governments in the years leading up to the First World War had long considered the area of Syria to be one of maximum importance. Indeed, some French policy makers of the late nineteenth century looked to Syria as a place where someday there might be an opportunity to press territorial claims that would result in the partition and ultimately the destruction of the Ottoman Empire. The British, however, felt at ease with the French in Syria as the idea of territorial acquisition was not one wholeheartedly supported by the French government as official policy. Rather, French investors through the Comité de Défense des Intérêts Francais en Orient, founded in 1911, called for an increased French presence in Syria in case of a partition, sparked by the collapse of Ottoman power, to preserve French business interests.[8] The government only felt compelled to consider this in an atmosphere where Ottoman power was on the decline in the wake of the 1912-1913 Balkan Wars. These wars resulted in the Ottoman loss of most of their European lands. The French government consequently began to doubt the long-term survival of the Ottoman Empire and thus worried about the potential disruption to its large business interests in Syria. Paris, however, believed despite the growing concern that partition

---

5   The acknowledgement of French interests in Syria culminated on 5 December 1912 with a British declaration from British Foreign Minister Sir Edward Grey that the British were not interested in Syria. See Jukka Nevakivi, *Britain, France, and the Middle East, 1914-1920* (London: Athlone Press, 1969), 8.
6   L. Bruce Fulton, "France and the End of the Ottoman Empire", in *The Great Powers and the End of the Ottoman Empire*, ed. Marian Kent (London: George Allen and Unwin), 141.
7   Zisser, 137.
8   For more information on this organization, see W.I. Shorrock, *French Imperialism in the Middle East: The Failure of Policy in Syria and Lebanon, 1900-1914* (Madison, WI: University of Wisconsin Press, 1976).

could potentially make matters worse through disruption of local French business interests as well as the Ottoman Imperial Bank. It could also allow other imperial powers to assert themselves within the empire as competitors, such as Germany. Only in the last months of peace did the matter seem increasingly within the realm of possibility. Thus on 6 November 1913 cabinet officials resolved to strengthen French influence in the case of partition.[9] French misgivings concerning partition would only harden in the opening months of the First World War in the wake of heavy losses suffered by the two French divisions that fought in the 1915 Gallipoli Campaign against the Ottoman Empire. Following this debacle, the French government by late July 1915 would finally call for the acquisition both of Cilicia and Syria at the close of the conflict.

The absence of government support for partition throughout the prewar years also existed in Germany, being the principal competitor of France in the Ottoman Empire. Indeed, the German relationship manifested itself in an alliance rather than a drive for partition. Berlin did not want the partition and destruction of the empire for both political and commercial reasons. German political overtures towards the Ottomans dated back at least to 1883 when a military mission under Generalmajor Otto Kaeler arrived in Istanbul to aid the Ottomans in introducing modern military reforms.[10] While the influence of this presence grew, so too did German economic activity spearheaded by the Berlin to Baghdad Railroad. Although incomplete in August 1914, it did carry around 60,000 passengers and 116,000 tons of freight annually.[11] This railroad progressively became a source of concern for the British as they feared that growing German influence within the Ottoman Empire might lead to its destabilization. Indeed, the construction of the railroad was the subject of several studies, conducted by the Committee of Imperial Defense, on the growing German influence in Ottoman lands. In 1905, the British stance concerning German influence was quite clear: under no circumstances should Germany be allowed to dominate the construction of the railroad line since this would directly affect British interests.[12] Connected to the railroad as well as to British concerns were the German banks that benefitted through the construction and finance of this railroad. Finally, the German armaments industry made increasingly greater sales to the Ottoman army in the years leading to the First World War. These activities were a reflection of German Kaiser

---

9   Fulton, 160.
10 Lieutenant-Colonel Baron Colmar von der Goltz succeeded General Major Otto Kaehler upon the latter's death in 1885. See David Bullock, *Allenby's War: The Palestine-Arabian Campaigns, 1916-1918* (London: Blandford Press, 1988), 12.
11 Ulrich Trumpener, "Germany and the End of the Ottoman Empire", in *The Great Powers and the End of the Ottoman Empire*, ed. Marian Kent (London: George Allen and Unwin), 117.
12 Great Britain, National Archives, Committee of Imperial Defense Memorandum, "The Berlin to Baghdad Railway", 26 January 1905, CAB 38/8/5. See also Great Britain, National Archives, Committee of Imperial Defense Memorandum, "The Berlin to Baghdad Railway: The Situation in November 1905", 1 November 1905, CAB 38/10/77.

Wilhelm II's policy of Weltpolitik, being the pursuit of German world power. The kaiser in the early twentieth century believed that the Ottomans might be a useful partner despite many of his senior government and military officials questioning the value of close political and military relations with them. This notion combined with the desire to protect German business interests within the Ottoman Empire led to the 2 August 1914 military alliance between Germany and the Ottoman Empire on the personal instructions of the kaiser.

The rising concern of the British over German influence in the Ottoman Empire was indicative of the fact that much of Britain's imperial concerns lay in the Mesopotamia rather than the Near East since the German funded railroad terminated in Baghdad. London believed that British supremacy in the regions of Mesopotamia and the Persian Gulf were critical to imperial communications and the defense of India, particularly in the wake of the imperial crisis with Russia in 1884 when St. Petersburg tried to expand into the region and thus threaten British interests in India. In addition, Mesopotamia was a growing strategic concern in the last years before the First World War owing to oil deposits in the region. British policymakers identified Mesopotamia as a region vital to the British Royal Navy, the protector of the British Empire since the navy began to construct oil-powered ships in 1906 and thus looked to the establishment of companies to extract the oil. Finally, the area also held the majority of British trading interests in the Ottoman Empire. In 1906, 79 percent of the total trade conducted into and out of the Persian Gulf was British and Indian. In that same year, 85 percent of all shipping plying the waters of the gulf was British and Indian. In order to protect these interests, Britain secured on 12 August 1913 an agreement with the Ottoman Empire that guaranteed British commercial interests versus rising German competition.[13]

Despite this agreement and the desire not to partition the Ottoman Empire, the British increasingly viewed the Turks as a potential threat to their interests in the Near East and in the last eight years before the war examined the hypothetical possibility of territorial expansion in the area. This reversal of past policy was the result of a 1906 dispute between Constantinople and London over the frontier between Egypt and the Ottoman Empire when the Sublime Porte challenged the 1892 agreement concerning the frontier. This agreement had established a line of demarcation running from Raffa to Aqaba with the Sinai Peninsula being under Ottoman rule but administered by British authorities. As a result of this crisis, between 1906 and 1909 the Committee of Imperial Defense increasingly examined the possibility of offensive operations against the Ottoman Empire although these, at first, did not include advances into the Sinai, Palestine, or Syria. The beginning of the consideration for military action came in the midst of the crisis when, on 9 May 1906, a report of the committee resolved that

---

13 Marian Kent, "Great Britain and the End of the Ottoman Empire, 1900-1923", in *The Great Powers and the End of the Ottoman Empire*, ed. Marian Kent (London: George Allen and Unwin), 179-180, 182.

the best measures to force an end to the dispute in favor of London was the occupation of the Ottoman Mediterranean islands of Lemnos, Mitylene, Tenedos, Imbros, and possibly Chios and Rhodes. Additional measures contemplated by the committee were the dispatch of warships to patrol near Istanbul and the western coast of the Persian Gulf.[14] In a subsequent meeting the committee resolved also to increase the garrison protecting Egypt and the Suez Canal in case of a Turkish attack across the Sinai Peninsula. As a portent of what was to come for the region, the members of the committee suggested that the troops should be sent from India.[15] None of these measures proved necessary as diplomats from both sides averted the crisis over the border.

The situation in 1906 starkly revealed to the British the vulnerability of the Suez Canal to possible incursion from the east.[16] During the crisis, the Committee of Imperial Defense identified only two avenues for the Ottomans to launch an attack against the Suez Canal. One of these was a route from Aqaba on the Red Sea to Suez. This southern route across the Sinai Peninsula encompassed a distance of 150 miles and was impractical owing to inadequate water supplies. Over the course of this distance was one 61-mile stretch between the water wells of Nakhl and Meibeiuk, which would prove impossible for a large army to traverse. As a result, the British deemed any Ottoman troop concentration at Aqaba to be impossible. The second route, however, was a cause of greater concern. This northern route, spanning 143 miles between Rafah and Kantara near the Suez Canal, had waterless stretches like the other route, but the gaps were ones of considerably less distance. The largest of these was 33 miles between Katia and Kantara. The author of the Committee of Imperial Defense memorandum examining this issue noted that this route was the one used by Napoleon Bonaparte during the French Revolutionary Wars for his Army of Egypt. This path offered greater possibility than the other. Even so, of the 33 miles between Katia and Kantara, 13 of them were soft sand, which would slow any advance and thus make the need for water more challenging since there were very few hard paths across the Sinai. Compounding this problem for the Ottomans would be trying to maneuver heavy artillery over the sand, which the author of the report noted was not a problem encountered by Napoleon since his army had no artillery. As a result, the Committee of Imperial Defense concluded that the Ottomans logistically could not mount an offensive over either path.

This conclusion, however, was not the end of concern over the vulnerability of the Suez Canal since the northern route offered at least the chance of an Ottoman assault. The 11 May 1906 memorandum of the Committee of Imperial Defense held that if this were to occur then "for the security and tranquility of Egypt, it is essential to preserve

---

14 Great Britain, National Archives, Committee of Imperial Defense Memorandum, "The Egyptian Frontier Question", 8 May 1906, CAB 38/11/19.
15 Great Britain, National Archives, Committee of Imperial Defense Memorandum, "The Egyptian Frontier Question", 11 May 1906, CAB 38/11/27, 3.
16 For full details of these two paths across the Sinai, see Great Britain, National Archives, CAB 38/11/19.

intact the strip of desert country, about 130 miles broad, which separates that frontier from the canal."[17] In the wake of this assessment some began to question the ability of British forces to hold this strip of land. Among them was Lieutenant-General Sir John French, a member of the Committee of Imperial Defense and Inspector-General of British Forces. He maintained that the Sinai desert should not be regarded as impassable, believing that within the next ten years the Turks might have the ability to cross the Sinai in large numbers with the logistical help of Germany, which was providing military assistance.[18] Within less than a year, French's view had a sufficient number of adherents to spark further discussion within the Imperial General Staff that looked to safeguarding the Suez Canal through measures other than defense through the seizure of Mediterranean islands held by the Ottomans. Director of Military Intelligence Major-General J.C. Ewart led this call in late 1906 through a recommendation observd:

> Great Britain in dealing with a power like Turkey could not afford merely to stand on the defensive. If we assume such an attitude, our prestige in the East would be gone. We must adopt a more active policy and find a theater of operations outside the Canal zone. Such a theater the General Staff consider can be found in Syria.[19]

With this conclusion the British were now envisioning action in an area within the Ottoman Empire in which London had previously had no interest, in order to protect the Suez Canal.

Despite the fact that officials at the time saw this course of action as merely a contingency plan should the Ottomans attack the Suez Canal, it was the beginning of British strategic planning against the Ottoman Empire. The plan that resulted held roughly the same objectives as those pursued by the British in during First World War that culminated with the Battle of Megiddo. One difference, however, was that the recommendation of the Imperial General Staff in 1906 was that they should conduct an amphibious invasion of Haifa, in modern-day Palestine, rather than advance through the Sinai Peninsula as during 1917-18. The plan envisioned securing the port for further operations into the interior of the Ottoman Empire. In 1907 the Committee of Imperial Defense embraced the idea proposed by the General Staff through the establishment of a sub-committee chaired by Lord Morley, the Secretary of State for India, to examine the requirements for the proper defense of the Suez Canal. This sub-committee echoed the call of 1906: "We should be obliged, whether

---

17 Great Britain, National Archives, CAB 38/11/19, 1.
18 Great Britain, National Archives, Committee of Imperial Defense Memorandum, "A Turco-German Invasion of Egypt", 6 July 1906, CAB 38/12/42.
19 Great Britain, National Archives, War Office Memorandum, "Coercion of Turkey by Military Operations in Syria-Haifa", WO 106/41, C3/14.

we like it or not, to adopt a more active policy to find a theater of operations...such a theater of operations can be found in Syria."[20]

To this end, the War Office sent several fact-finding missions to Syria between 1907 and the outbreak of the First World War to gather as much intelligence as possible on the areas of modern-day Lebanon, Palestine, Israel, and Syria, and the logistical net of the Ottoman Army in order to facilitate war planning. One of the first reconnaissance missions was conducted beginning in March 1907 by Lieutenant-Colonel Francis Richard Maunsell, a former military attaché to Constantinople. Published in June 1908 for the Imperial General Staff and entitled "Reconnaissance of Syria from the Coast Eastwards," it served as the basis for more detailed planning of the potential invasion of Syria by British forces.[21] This report identified potential landing sites and avenues of attack into the interior of Syria. One scenario envisioned a landing in Haifa with an advance to Derra, which lay on the Hejaz railway that ran south into Arabia. The other was a landing in Beirut with an advance to the area around Tripoli and Homs. In both instances Maunsell meticulously described roads and railroads as the British looked to not only using these as avenues of advance, but to deny them to the Ottomans.

The War Office subsequently used Maunsell's report to create plans for operations in case of war with the Ottoman Empire. The first created by the War Office in June 1908 and entitled "General Scheme for the Invasion of Syria by an Expeditionary Force," called for an amphibious landing in Haifa as suggested by Maunsell, but designated Damascus as the ultimate objective rather than Derra.[22] Subsequent plans put forth by the General Staff and the Committee of Imperial Defense upheld the landing site of Haifa with the intermediate objectives of Nazareth and the area around the Sea of Galilee. These plans increasingly benefitted from more intelligence gathering in the region of Syria, one of the last being an expedition between December 1913 and March 1914 led by T.E. Lawrence, whose future exploits culminating in the Battle of Megiddo would earn him great fame.[23]

None of these schemes became official plans for operations against the Ottoman Empire before 1914, although they did prove valuable in terms of the war. The impetus to explore the matter had always been in anticipation of an attack on the Suez Canal in the wake of the 1906 border dispute. In addition, amidst rising tension in Europe, General Sir John French, who assumed the office of Chief of the Imperial General Staff in 1912, believed that the primary consideration in the event of a war was to

---

20   Great Britain, National Archives, Circular submitted to the members of the Morley Committee, WO 106/42, C3/26.
21   See Yigal Sheffy, *British Military Intelligence in the Palestine Campaign, 1914-1918* (London: Frank Cass, 1998), 25-26.
22   Great Britain, National Archives, War Office Memorandum, "General Scheme for the Invasion of Syria by an Expeditionary Force", June 1908, WO 106/43, C3/29.
23   For information on this fact finding mission, see David Garnett, ed., *The Letters of T.E. Lawrence* (New York: Doubleday, Doran, 1939), 162-168.

focus British resources on the European continent. As a result, French opined that "the remoter possibility of an attack on Egypt ought not to occupy the time of the General Staff."[24] Given this stance and the deteriorating situation in Europe, by 1914 all plans for operations against the Ottomans were shelved with the focus being placed by the British on the urgent matter of defending their French allies. Even so, the planning of operations against the Ottomans did prove important during the First World War. Yigal Sheffy, a noted scholar in the field of intelligence, observes that until 1914, the British had no institutionalized intelligence agency functioning on a permanent basis in the Ottoman Empire. With the exception of the fact finding missions undertaken by the War Office such as Maunsell's and Lawrence's, the majority of intelligence came from only the British Embassy in Constantinople with its 45 consulates and vice-consulates.[25] As a result, the intelligence collected on the Ottoman railroad and road systems, the Ottoman Army, and the terrain of Syria through individuals such as Maunsell and Lawrence proved invaluable to the British when they considered operations versus the Ottoman Empire in the context of the First World War.

The entry of the Ottoman Empire into the First World War as a member of the Central Powers, along with Germany and Austria-Hungary, resulted from talks that began in the last weeks of peace. The Ottoman alliance was, at first, the result of the Porte's perceived need for a closer relationship with a European power to preserve the empire. Most of the Young Turks that governed the Ottoman Empire believed that an alliance with Germany served best to protect the empire from becoming "Russia's vassal" as the territorial interests of the Russians had cost the empire lands in the Caucasus in the pre-war years. Also, Minister of War Enver Pasha and Minister of the Interior Mehmet Talaat, being two of the most powerful members of the Young Turks, believed that an alliance with Germany was the better choice due to its military power and their conviction that the Central Powers would win the war.[26] Overtures to the Germans resulted with a formal proposal from Istanbul to Berlin on 28 July 1914 that culminated in the 2 August 1914 alliance between Germany and the Ottoman Empire. There was very little concerning definitive war aims for the empire in this first agreement. It called for the Ottoman Empire to declare war for Germany should the latter country become involved in a war with Russia, which had already come to pass the day before. As a result of the signing of this document the Ottomans became an ally of Germany. The treaty stressed the secret nature of the relationship and at first the Porte publicly declared the neutrality of the empire despite German calls for activation of the alliance. Grand Vizier Sait Halim, who did not want war and supported the Entente more than Germany, was hesitant despite the signing of the alliance to enter the conflict. He only honored a pledge for general mobilization of the

24 Sheffy, *British Military Intelligence in the Palestine Campaign*, 27.
25 See Yigal Sheffy, "British Intelligence in the Middle East, 1900-1918: How Much Do We Know?", *Intelligence and National Security* 17, no. 1 (Spring 2002), 33-52.
26 Richard F. Hamilton and Holger Herwig, *Decisions for War, 1914-1917* (Cambridge: Cambridge University Press, 2004), 159.

Ottoman Army. At the same time, Enver Pasha tried to assure the Russians that the mobilization was not directed at them, even going so far as to offer a thinning out of Ottoman troops along the trans-Caucasian border in return for Russian aid to help the Ottomans recapture the Aegean Islands from Greece and Western Thrace from Bulgaria, both being lost in the 1912 Balkan War.

This overture, which came to naught, was the first instance where the Ottomans looked to clear goals in the context of the war. The original treaty was subsequently modified on 6 August 1914 in an atmosphere where the Porte allowed the entry of the German battle cruiser *Goeben* and light cruiser *Breslau* into the Dardanelles to escape a British squadron in the Mediterranean. Istanbul sought to quell the concerns of the British and French over this move by declaring that they would purchase the ships upon their arrival for use in the Ottoman Navy.[27] In exchange, the grand vizier asked the Germans to accept six proposals that modified the existing agreement. These included the abolition of the capitulations that exempted outside powers, like the French in Syria, from Ottoman taxes. It also called for help regaining lost territories of the empire, such as the Aegean Islands if Greece entered the war as a hostile power, and a slight redrawing of the Turkish eastern border with Russia. Finally, the Turks called for a war indemnity. By 6 August 1914 the Ottomans were looking largely to economic aggrandizement rather than territorial concessions in order to strengthen an empire deeply in debt.[28] The Germans immediately agreed to these stipulations out of concern for the safe haven of their warships. Even so, the Porte remained largely uncommitted to war, favoring armed neutrality. This situation only changed on 29 October 1914 when the German warships *Goeben* and *Breslau*, staffed by their German crews but under the Turkish flag, bombarded Russian ships and port facilities at Sevastopol. The operation appears sanctioned only by Enver Pasha, who issued orders allowing offensive operations without going through the existing chain of command.[29] This act resulted in a Russian declaration of war on the Ottoman Empire on 2 November 1914 followed by declarations from Britain and France.

The entry of the Ottoman Empire into the war as a Central Power posed great problems for the Entente, particularly the British. In terms of the alliance as a whole, the most pressing problem was the closure of the Dardanelles and as a result the blockage of the Black Sea as an avenue for badly needed supply to Russia. This situation meant that the only secure route for Allied supplies to flow to Russia was an overland route that ran through neutral Sweden, which was always a source of concern for the Allies as the Swedes, despite being neutral, were sympathetic to Germany.[30] More

---

27 See Dan Van der Vat, *The Ship that Changed the World: The Escape of the Goeben to the Dardanelles in 1914* (Bethesda, MD: Adler and Adler, 1986).
28 Edward Erickson, *Ordered to Die: A History of the Ottoman Army in the First World War* (Westport, Conn.: Greenwood Press, 2001), 27.
29 Erickson, *Ordered to Die*, 36.
30 Eric W. Osborne, *Britain's Economic Blockade of Germany, 1914-1919* (London: Frank Cass, 2004), 67.

specifically for the British, the other serious concern was the threat that the Ottoman Empire posed to the Suez Canal with the possibility of an offensive launched through the Sinai Peninsula. This possibility had been the impetus of the first planning for military action against the Ottomans in the wake of the 1906 border dispute. The strategic need to defend the canal led to the siphoning off of troops to Egypt that could have been deployed to the Western Front against Germany.

The latter threat to the canal was certainly one that could not materialize immediately upon Ottoman entry into the war. The 2 August 1914 alliance with Germany had only led to a state of benevolent neutrality for the Ottomans towards the Germans. As a result, the mobilization of the Ottoman Army at first was purely defensive in nature. Even if this had not been the case, the Ottomans were also handicapped from the outset in terms of launching offensive operations by the very poor state of supply to their mobilizing army. Those units closest to Istanbul suffered the least, but even these were greatly retarded in their efforts to mobilize. The I Corps of the Ottoman Army, based in Thrace, needed 19 days to mobilize at least on paper, but in reality it took 64 days to make the corps combat ready. Among the problems cited by the officers of I Corps were a lack of artillery horses and general transport.[31] Shortages such as these and consequently in the supply of ammunition and basic items such as uniforms became more acute for Ottoman units that were outside the region of Turkey, such as Mesopotamia, Syria, and Arabia.

These problems hampered the performance of the Ottoman Army throughout the war. A chief handicap of the force was the empire's logistical net, which was not capable of adequately supplying the far-flung units of the empire. A critical problem was the railroad system which was not designed for the support of armies in time of war. These railroads had not been built by the Ottomans themselves, but rather by the European imperial powers that in the pre-war world had sought out business interests within the Ottoman realm. France and Germany accounted for much of the railroad construction owing to their interests in Syria and in the Berlin to Baghdad Railroad, respectively. As a result, there were three different gauges of track within the Ottoman Empire: standard gauge of 4.4 meters, 1.05-meter gauge, and one meter gauge.[32] The main line, comprised of standard gauge, ran from Haidar Pasha on the eastern shore of the Bosporus at Istanbul and was part of the Berlin to Baghdad Railroad. It ran through Musliye Junction just north of Aleppo. There, the line branched off with the main line continuing to Syria as far south as Rayak while the other led to Mesopotamia. There was also a line that ran from Homs to Tripoli built to the same gauge. Collectively these railroad lines ran a length of 240 miles. The rest of the lines, however, were made primarily of 1.05-meter gauge and spanned 1,125 miles of the empire. Much of this was in the

---

31 Erickson, *Ordered to Die*, 40-41.
32 David L. Bullock, *Allenby's War: The Palestine-Arabian Campaigns, 1916-1918* (London: Blandford, 1988), 17.

region of Syria and Arabia. Finally, there was a French-built line spanning 25 miles between Jaffa and Jerusalem.[33]

The problems associated with these lines were many. The first of these was that the main line that ran from Haidar Pasha had to serve both the Syrian and Mesopotamian theaters of war, making it extremely difficult to convey adequate supply to either area. Indeed, the size of the railroad in relation to that of the empire was totally inadequate. In 1914, the railroad of the Ottoman Empire measured 3,578 miles for an area of 930,506 square miles. By way of comparison, in the same year the railroad of Germany extended 39,768 miles to cover 208,495 square miles.[34] Compounding this problem was geography as the Ottomans had to contend with railroads that ran through mountainous terrain. In the case of the main line, this resulted in a break in two portions on the way to Aleppo: one being at the Taurus Mountains and the other at the Amanus Mountains. In each instance, the Ottomans had to offload the supplies, travel by road through the mountains, and then reload the supplies onto the trains. An additional transshipment at Rayak added to the difficulty of transport since the standard gauge line ended there as the track pushed into southern Palestine. This overall situation greatly hampered Ottoman supply to its forces in Palestine. The Ottomans were largely reliant for logistical supply to Palestine on a 1,275-mile multi-gauge railroad that ran from Haidar Pasha to the front at either Gaza or Beersheba broken in five places by problems with terrain and non-standard gauge lines.[35] This greatly slowed transport. Throughout most of the war until shortly before the armistice, when new construction partially alleviated the problem, it took anywhere from a month to six weeks for reinforcements to get from Istanbul to the front in Palestine. Once there, if the railroad was congested from offloading at Rayak, troops had to march some 250 miles to reach the southern Palestine theater and were thus exhausted when they arrived.[36] Another factor that decreased the effectiveness of the Ottoman logistical net was the fact that there were very few metalled roads in Palestine of Syria, being roads with a level surface made of pieces of fine stone. If troops and supplies had to be transported by truck or horse the Turks relied on a system of largely dirt roads that became impassable during the rainy season in the area.

Still more problems affected the Turkish ability to supply the troops of their vast empire. Associated with the condition of the railways was a great shortage of rolling stock, fuel for use on them, and poor leadership. In 1914, the Ottoman Empire had at its disposal 280 engines, 720 passenger cars, and 4,500 freight cars of varying gauge. Only 75 percent of these were operational at any given time in an atmosphere where there were few, well-stocked repair fascilities.[37] The engines that pulled these cars

---

33 For details on these railroad lines, see Archibald C. Wavell, *The Palestine Campaigns* (London: Constable, 1941), 11.
34 Ahmed Emin Yalman, *Turkey in the World War* (New Haven: Conn.: Yale University Press, 1930), 85.
35 Wavell, 12.
36 Wavell, 13.
37 Yalman, 93.

suffered severely with a shortage of fuel for much of the war. In the years leading to the First World War, the Ottomans produced less coal than Germany, Great Britain, France, or Italy. Whilst in 1914 the Ottomans produced 846,000 tons of coal in the empire, the production of Germany was 277,000,000 tons.[38] The Ottoman Empire relied consequently on overseas supply, chiefly from Great Britain. In 1910 Great Britain accounted for 94 percent of Ottoman coal imports in order to address the relatively low amount of domestically produced coal.[39] Upon the outbreak of war, the supply from Great Britain naturally ended, but in addition the Ottomans had trouble securing additional avenues of overseas supply due to a naval blockade imposed by the allied navies that cut off most of its ports to the rest of the world. In 1914, over 70 percent of the Ottoman import trade entered primarily Istanbul and Haidar Pasha, Smyrna, Beirut, and Alexandretta. All could be easily blockaded by a naval force in the Mediterranean. The rest of the above amount flowed into Trebizond and Baghdad: these two avenues could be easily stemmed.[40] As a result, the Ottomans had to rely heavily on wood to power their locomotives, which was far less efficient than coal and not in adequate supply for the war effort. British intelligence noted in a report at the end of 1915 that: "Owing to the shortage of coal all trains S. of Aleppo run on wood. Hence great reduction in speed, and numerous halts to take in fresh supplies of fuel."[41] The same report exhibits the insatiable need for wood in this atmosphere. By the end of 1915, "The Turkish authorities were compelled to cut down all olive trees round Aleppo, Beirut, and Lebanon for fuel.[42] By the time of the Battle of Megiddo in September 1918, wood supplies were low enough that it was hindering the operation of locomotives. On 15 September 1918, four days before Megiddo, a captured Turkish document from the Railway Transport Department at Aleppo stated that "On account of scarcity of wood, No. 1751 train left with one engine on 14 Sept. The load of the train was reduced by half on its return ... Today No. 1751 train has not left owing to lack of wood."[43] Clearly, the Ottoman Empire was not prepared to address the necessities of modern, industrialized warfare. Finally, compounding the material

---

38   Press Publishing, *The World Almanac and Encyclopedia, 1914* (New York: Press Publishing, 1913), 244.
39   Archibald Bell, *A History of the Blockade of Germany and the Countries Associated with Her in the Great War: Austria-Hungary, Bulgaria, and Turkey, 1914-1918* (London: HMSO, 1961), 369.
40   Bell, 371.
41   Great Britain, National Archives, Political and Economic Intelligence Summaries, April 1918-Spetember 1918, "Number 4 Report, Economic Section, General Staff Intelligence, GHQ, EEF", WO 157/735, 33.
42   Great Britain, National Archives, Political and Economic Intelligence Summaries, April 1918-Spetember 1918, "Number 4 Report, Economic Section, General Staff Intelligence, GHQ, EEF", WO 157/735, 33.
43   Great Britain, National Archives, Political and Economic Intelligence Summaries, April 1918-Spetember 1918, "GHQ Intelligence Summary for 24 hours ending 2200-28th September, 1918" 28 September 1918, WO 157/731, 2.

problems was the leadership of the supply effort. The ability to secure proper supplies suffered in part from the inefficiency of Turkish officials and a penchant for bribery within the system.[44]

Ottoman finances as well as a meager industrial base further hampered the empire's ability to properly supply its army. The Ottoman Empire entered the First World War heavily indebted to foreign bondholders. By 1914, thirty percent of the Porte's annual budget serviced the national debt in an atmosphere where between 1911 and 1913 the national debt averaged thirty-four million Turkish Pounds.[45] The state of Ottoman industry hindered its ability to provide for its armed forces. In an age where warfare depended on industry, the Ottomans produced precious little steel and iron since the economic base of the empire remained largely agricultural. The few factories that produced arms and ammunition were all located in Istanbul and could not provide adequately for a protracted war. The entire industrial production of the empire in military terms consisted of one artillery and small arms plant, one shell and bullet facility, and one gunpowder plant.[46] The poor productive capacity of these few factories led to a series of agreements between the Ottoman Empire and Germany over the course of the First World War in which the Germans provided equipment that included artillery, rifles, machine guns, ammunition, and aircraft.

Finally, the Ottomans also struggled militarily with an army that was still in the process of being rebuilt as a result of heavy losses sustained in the 1912 and 1913 Balkan Wars. In these conflicts, only six of the 43 infantry divisions of the empire did not participate in combat. Of this overall total, the wars destroyed fourteen infantry divisions and led to 250,000 casualties.[47] These losses shattered the Ottoman Army since many corps had been dissolved while many infantry divisions had wide differences in their fighting strengths. As a result, the Ottomans found themselves in a situation that demanded a large military rebuilding program. Aiding them in this effort was the German Military Mission led by Major General Liman von Sanders.

These efforts certainly improved the condition of the Turkish army by the outbreak of the war, although many in the British military as well as those working for the British as intelligence gatherers discounted the Ottomans as a viable fighting force. In October 1913, Colonel Henry Wilson, the British Army's Director of Military Operations, characterized the Ottoman Army as "not a serious modern army…no sign of adaption to western thoughts and methods. The army is ill-officered and in rags."[48] Echoing this sentiment were those individuals who gathered intelligence data for the British on the state of the Ottoman Army as well as the empire in general.

---

44 H. Pirie Gordon, *A Brief Record of the Advance of the Egyptian Expeditionary Force* (London, HMSO: 1919), 128.
45 Yalman, 93.
46 Erickson, *Ordered to Die*, 16-17.
47 Erickson, *Ordered to Die*, 10.
48 Edward Erickson, *Ottoman Army Effectiveness in First World War: A Comparative Study* (London: Routledge, 2007), 7.

Among these was Philip Graves, a *London Times* correspondent for Cairo and Istanbul who reported to the British War Office concerning the Ottomans. His report of 10 November 1914 contained the assessment that "Taking the Turkish Army as a whole, I should say it was militia only moderately trained and composed of tough, but slow-witted peasants liable to panic before the unexpected."[49] Neither of these assessments is entirely accurate. The first of these was uttered at a time when the Ottoman reorganization plan was in its infancy, while the second greatly discounts the strides made with the help of the German Military Mission. Liman von Sanders helped to not only rebuild Ottoman formations destroyed by the Balkan Wars, but he also oversaw training modeled on the German Army, which had existed in the years before the wars. In addition, a chief facet of the plan was the staffing of several infantry divisions and corps of the army with German officers to offset a key problem of the lack of adequately trained junior officers since many of their number had been consumed by the conflict and could not be easily replaced.

These efforts greatly improved the state of the Ottoman Army, although by the outbreak of the First World War, the general assessment of the Ottoman Army as one unprepared for war was still accurate. In August 1914, of the 36 Turkish infantry divisions mobilized for action 22 were either new or had gone through a redeployment in the months leading up to the Great War. These units consequently were not fully prepared for combat, the problem being that the First World War opened too soon after the Balkan Wars for the reorganization plan to have been fully effective.[50] In addition, the infantry divisions that did exist were under-strength. In August 1914, the strength of Ottoman infantry divisions averaged 4,000 men rather than the prescribed 10,000 necessary to make them prepared for war.[51] They were also unprepared given supply shortages that existed at the outbreak of the conflict owing to the poor state of Ottoman industry. Ottoman divisions lacked the proper amount of artillery, small arms, machine guns, and ammunition. The chief deficiencies of these at the outbreak of the war were machine guns and ammunition. The Ottoman General Staff believed that several thousand machine guns were needed to address shortages where many battalions had none of the weapons at all. In terms of issued ammunition, each man carried 150 rounds of small arms ammunition available whilst the entire army depended on a stockpile of 200,000,000 rifle cartridges.[52]

Despite the host of problems, the Ottomans did, however, devise plans for operations against the Allied powers. The Primary Campaign Plan for the Turkish Army was completed in April 1914 before either the alliance with Germany or the outbreak of the war. The plan was a defensive one in a situation where the Ottoman Army had to safeguard multiple fronts of the empire, namely Thrace, Caucasia, Mesopotamia,

49 Erickson, *Ottoman Army Effectiveness in First World War: A Comparative Study*, 7.
50 Erickson, *Ordered to Die*, 11.
51 Sheffy, *British Military Intelligence in the Palestine Campaign*, 34. See also Erickson, *Ordered to Die*, 7.
52 Erickson, *Ordered to Die*, 8.

and Syria. Of these, the plan focused on the defense of Thrace and Caucasia as the Turkish General Staff believed that the empire's principal opponents would be Bulgaria and Greece, in keeping with the experience of the Balkan Wars, and Russia. Thrace was the most important front given the strategic importance of Istanbul. As a result, mobilization planning under the original Primary Campaign Plan called for the location of the majority of the army in Thrace and western Anatolia. Indeed, the plan called for the removal of the entire regular army from Syria as well as significant portion of it from Mesopotamia for redeployment to the European front.

Only at the outbreak of the First World War did the plan change as the Turkish General Staff believed events that had unfolded in the early weeks of the conflict required its revision. The British reaction to these revised plans once they were implemented would culminate in the Battle of Megiddo. By late August 1914 a secret military alliance with Bulgaria negated the threat posed to Thrace while the possibility of Russian offensives in Caucasia declined as a result of the large-scale operations of czarist forces against Germany and Austria-Hungary. In addition, the Turks perceived the likelihood of hostilities breaking out against Great Britain given their alliance with Germany. This threatened Turkish interests both in Syria and Mesopotamia. As a result, on 6 September 1914 the general staff significantly revised the plan.[53] The new scheme turned away from a mostly defensive deployment and envisioned one designed for offensive operations on multiple fronts. While the majority of the army remained in Thrace to protect Istanbul and possibly conduct joint operations with the Bulgarians versus either Greece or Serbia, Ottoman forces would launch attacks against the Russians in Caucasia. The other aspects of the plan dealt with the new threat posed by Great Britain. Not only would Turkish forces in Mesopotamia apply pressure to British interests in Afghanistan and India, but Turkish forces would prepare an attack against Egypt. The objective for the latter offensive was to threaten the Suez Canal and thus Britain's supply line to India. It also negated the threat of a British amphibious assault launched from Egypt. The Turks believed that Britain might launch such an assault between Gaza and Alexandretta thus threatening Palestine. Indeed, the scenario envisioned by the Turks was exactly that which the British considered in the pre-war years should the Ottomans attack the Suez Canal. The new plan consequently assigned the Ottoman Fourth Army in Palestine with launching an attack on Egypt.

The revision of the Turkish war plans that ultimately made Syria and Palestine a theater of operations unfolded in an atmosphere where the British government hoped that the Ottomans would remain neutral despite their alliance with Germany. While Major General Julian Byng, the commander of Britain's Army of Occupation in Egypt, made preparations to evacuate the eastern Sinai in the event of an Ottoman assault, British intelligence in August and early September suggested no offensive

---

53 For additional coverage of the Primary Campaign Plan, see Erickson, *Ordered to Die*, 39. See also Sheffy, *British Military Intelligence in the Palestine Campaign*, 35.

troop movements in Palestine. Despite a growing number of intelligence reports over the first three weeks of October that detailed large scale troop movements southwards from Aleppo and Mesopotamia to Syria and Palestine, British intelligence explained it as a defensive move by the Ottomans. The British believed that the Ottomans, in the event that they found themselves at war, wanted to safeguard Palestine and Syria against possible amphibious landings that might threaten these areas.[54] Such a conclusion should not come as a great surprise, given that this scenario was exactly what the British had planned in the pre-war years for their defense of Egypt and the Suez Canal versus Ottoman incursions. These October reports merely supported London's view of the Ottomans since the outbreak of the war. This caused them to withdraw all regular troops from Egypt for use on the Western Front and replace them with imperial and territorial troops for defense of the canal. To these troops fell the duty of defending Britain's lifeline to the east upon the 2 November British declaration of war against the Ottoman Empire. This situation led to the British implementation of a strategic plan that shifted decisively London's stance as the protector of the Ottoman Empire to one that envisioned offensive operations with the ultimate goal of partitioning the empire for imperial gain. The Battle of Megiddo would serve as the culminating offensive to achieve that aim.

54 Sheffy, *British Military Intelligence in the Palestine Campaign*, 41.

2

Allied Shift from the Defense of Egypt to Offensives into Palestine Strategic and Political Motivations

The Ottomans, despite their mobilization difficulties upon the outbreak of the war, endeavored to quickly launch an assault on British defenses around the Suez Canal. The objective was not the outright seizure of the canal, but to block access through it by sending troops across it in order to seize the town of Ismailia on the western bank of the canal. The Ottoman General Staff also hoped that success in the offensive might spark a Muslim revolt of Egyptians against their British occupiers. Istanbul entrusted this operation to the 80,000-man Fourth Army based in Damascus under the command of General Djemal Pasha. A member of the Young Turks, Djemal had served as the Ottoman Minister of Marine in 1913 before becoming military governor of Syria on the outbreak of the war. Throughout December 1914, Djemal positioned troops in Beersheba for an assault and placed them under the command of German Colonel Kress von Kressenstein. This appointment serves as an early illustration of the enduring German presence in the command echelons of the Ottoman Army throughout the war in keeping with their pre-war involvement with Istanbul through their military mission. Kressenstein had served in the pre-war years as part of the German Military Mission and upon its outbreak became chief of staff for the Ottoman VIII Corps within the Fourth Army.

By early January 1915, the Ottomans had assembled 22,000 men for an assault across the Sinai to the Suez Canal. Kressenstein began this assault on 4 January with the occupation of Nakhl within the Sinai and subsequently pressed forward in a ten-day march across the peninsula. This was a truly impressive feat given the geography of the Sinai and its relative lack of water and food. To offset the latter two problems, Kressenstein's force marched with 5,000 camels carrying water and subsisted only on dates, olives, and biscuits. They also took advantage of wells found along their march, so that the force arrived in relatively good order along a wide front for its attack on the Suez Canal.

By late January 1915, the British defenses which might repel an Ottoman attack on the Suez Canal were not elaborate. The key to the defense of the area proved to be the 200-foot wide canal itself. Defensive positions on both banks of the canal buttressed the defense, with 18 of these being located on the eastern bank. These latter positions were mostly for the debarkation of troops for defense and counterattack. Supplementing the land contingent of the defense were British and French warships stationed in the canal.[1] The defense of the canal zone by this time was entrusted to divisions under the command of Lieutenant General Sir John Maxwell. He was well-suited to the defense of the region, as he had served both in 1882 in the operation that had given Britain informal control of Egypt and subsequently in the Egyptian Army where he saw extensive service in the Sudan. Between 1908 and 1912, Maxwell served further as the commander of all British forces in Egypt before being promoted to lieutenant general and being relieved of command. Recalled to active service in his former post by early November 1914, Maxwell presided in January 1915 over an Egypt garrisoned by over 150,000 troops from India, Australia, New Zealand, and Great Britain.[2]

Despite being greatly outnumbered, the attack launched by the Ottomans on the night of 2 February 1915 had some initial success. The attack, however, ultimately failed as a British observation post identified Ottoman troops trying to cross over the canal in pontoon boats. From this point forward, the outcome of the attack was not in doubt. By the late afternoon of 3 February when Djemal Pasha ordered Kressenstein to retreat, the Ottomans had suffered 192 dead, 381 wounded, and 787 missing or captured.[3] British losses numbered far fewer with the majority being Indian troops. Repulsing the attack cost four killed and 18 wounded for British troops while Indians suffered 25 dead and 110 wounded.[4]

While the losses sustained by the Ottomans were paltry in comparison to the size of their force, the British found through reconnaissance on the east bank of the Suez Canal in the aftermath of the battle, that the Turks had abandoned their positions. The reason was logistical since the first attack cost the Ottomans their boats and made any further crossing of the canal impossible. As a result, by the middle of February 1915 the bulk of Ottoman troops involved in the assault had been pulled back to Gaza with only one division remaining at Beersheba. This retreat led to a situation where the Turks launched only harassing attacks through the remainder of the year, as they diverted a great many of their troops to Gallipoli to counter Allied operations in the Dardanelles and the Gallipoli peninsula. Only in June 1916 did they launch another major operation. The British repulsed it as well and it proved to be the last threat posed by the Turks to the Suez Canal in the war.

---

1   For details on these defenses, see Roger Ford, *Eden to Armageddon: World War I in the Middle East* (New York: Pegasus Books, 2010), 299. See also David R. Woodward, *Hell in the Holy Land: World War I in the Middle East* (Lexington, KY: University of Kentucky Press, 2006), 15-16.
2   Edward Erickson, *Ordered to Die: A History of the Ottoman Army in the First World War* (Westport, Conn.: Greenwood Press, 2001), 71.
3   Erickson, *Ordered to Die*, 71.
4   Woodward, *Hell in the Holy Land*, 15.

Maxwell's initial successful defense, however, was one of the few occasions in 1915 for celebration for the Allies. By 1915 Allied strategy towards the Ottomans rested on two other goals besides the defense of the Suez Canal and both these met with disaster. The first of these was the opening of the Dardanelles. While in possession of this waterway, the Ottomans were able to deny this avenue to the Allies as a way to supply Russia, which was chronically short of supplies for much of the war. British attempts to secure the Dardanelles in 1915 met with unmitigated disaster, primarily through the costly failure of the Gallipoli campaign that unfolded between 25 April 1915 and 9 January 1916. The second strategic goal was the seizure of Mesopotamia which had oil fields critical to the Turks and of use to the Allies. There were some British successes when the British seized the oil fields of Mesopotamia in 1915. Even so, by the end of the year efforts to follow up this success with an assault on Baghdad were checked by Ottoman forces and ultimately led to the disaster at Kut al Amara the following year, where the Indian 6th Division finally surrendered on 22 April 1916 after a prolonged siege.

British and imperial forces bore the majority of the European commitment against the Ottoman Empire as the great majority of the French Army fought on the Western Front. The end of 1915 saw the British largely taking a defensive posture in the Middle East while the primary strategic focus, and consequently the majority of military resources, were dedicated to the Western European front against Germany.

This defensive stance, however, indicated a shift in British grand strategy toward the Ottoman Empire that was echoed by their French allies in the months before and during both the Gallipoli Campaign and the advances into Mesopotamia. Increasingly, the British abandoned their previous policy of maintaining the territorial integrity of the Ottoman Empire. One of the first indications of this shift in British circles occurred on 9 November 1914 when Prime Minister Herbert Asquith publicly predicted the partition of the Ottoman Empire at the end of the war.[5] Also in November came calls in keeping with the nationalist movement of Zionism for a Jewish homeland in Palestine following the partition of the empire. There was also French diplomatic correspondence about asking the Russian stance on France pressing territorial claims in Syria. With the exception of Germany, these powers represented all those with an interest in the Ottoman Empire in the pre-war period.

Despite his prediction, however, Prime Minister Asquith and his war council were at first divided over partition of the empire. At a meeting on 19 March 1915 of the cabinet, Foreign Minister Sir Edward Grey posed the question of whether territorial acquisition at the expense of the Ottoman Empire would strengthen the British Empire or not. Disagreement over the issue led to the establishment in April of the de Bunsen Committee, named after its chairman Sir Maurice de Bunsen, and charged with examining British interests in the Middle East. The final report, issued in June

---

5   Jukka Nevakivi, *Britain, France, and the Arab Middle East, 1914-1920* (London: Athlone Press, 1969), 13.

1915, concluded that the establishment of zones of interest between the great powers was preferable to outright partition. That conclusion was primarily the result of the cabinet's reluctance to meet Russia's demands in the case of partition, since on 4 March the tsar had demanded that Russia receive Istanbul and the Dardanelles Straits as part of any partition agreement.[6] Even so, the de Bunsen Committee's report was a clear indication of a shift in British foreign policy towards dominance of a portion of the Ottoman Empire for their own imperial gain in the postwar world. The scheme for zones of influence was one of four plans produced by the committee and called for informal British control of an area that encompassed Palestine, southern Syria, and Mesopotamia. The northern line of demarcation for the British sphere stretched from Acre and ran just south of Damascus to Ruwandiz. The southern line of demarcation stretched from Aqaba to Kuwait. Also under this arrangement France would receive northern Syria as a zone of interest while Russia gained informal control of Istanbul and the Dardanelles Straits.[7] In addition to this plan, the committee also drew up one map in its report that envisioned the partition of the Ottoman Empire. Under this scheme, Britain would lay direct claim to the same zone as that demarcated in the plan for informal control.[8]

The reason for an emphasis on control of this region was clearly imperial. The construction of a railroad running through this zone from Mesopotamia to the Mediterranean would allow access to the oil fields of Mosul and Kirkuk, which would help to address Britain's need for oil as the Royal Navy required this with its shift to oil-fired ships. Indeed, the acquisition of Mesopotamia was far more important to the members of the War Council than that of Palestine as long as the port of Haifa could be secured in the Mediterranean. The strategic vulnerability of Britain in terms of oil was starkly revealed during 1914-18. Throughout the conflict, Britain was dependent on the United States for 80 percent of its oil requirements.[9] In view of the conclusions of the de Bunsen Committee, the War Council clearly appreciated this problem.

The de Bunsen Committee's report served as a foundation for future talks with the European parties that had a stake in the fate of the Middle East in the postwar world. These talks widened in the months after the report was released to include negotiations with the Arabs within the Ottoman Empire. British concerns towards the Arabs were two-fold. The first of these was that the destruction of the Ottoman Empire would lead to the end of the traditional seat of Islam and possibly produce instability both in the Near East and in areas of the British Empire that held large

---

6   E.L. Woodward and Rohan Butler, *Documents on British Foreign Policy, 1919-1939*, first series, volume 4 (London: HMSO, 1952), 635-636.
7   Great Britain, National Archives, War Council Memorandum, "Report of the Committee on Asiatic Turkey", June 1915, CAB 42/3.
8   Great Britain, National Archives, War Council Memorandum, "Report of the Committee on Asiatic Turkey", June 1915, CAB 42/3, 26.
9   Clifford Kiracofe, Jr., *Dark Crusade: Christian Zionism and US Foreign Policy* (London: I.B. Taurus, 2009), 73.

Muslim populations, specifically India. In this atmosphere, members of the War Council such as Secretary of War Field Marshal Lord Kitchener advocated the creation of a new Arab caliphate in Arabia although this would do little to assuage Indian Muslims since the majority of them were pro-Turk. The second consideration was that advocacy of a new Arab caliphate would induce a rebellion of Arabs within the Ottoman Empire that might weaken their war effort. The first overtures to the Arabs that took both of these considerations into account occurred before the war, although they were quite vague. In 1912-13 Kitchener, as consul general of Egypt, approached the Hashemite Sharif of Mecca Ali ibn Hussein promising support for an independent Arab state in the event of a successful Arab uprising versus the Ottomans. At that time, Kitchener was convinced that the destruction of the Ottoman Empire was imminent. He consequently sought to secure support from Arabs as a friendly relationship with them would improve security for both Egypt and India.[10] Kitchener continued to champion the idea of an Arab caliphate once he became secretary of war. During the March war council meetings that led to the de Bunsen Committee report, he advocated the same course of action.[11] The field marshal attached special importance to the establishment of a friendly Arab regime in order for Britain to secure its interests in Mesopotamia. Kitchener's stance was certainly not one that was universally advocated by members of the British government. Its chief opponents were Viceroy of India Lord Hardinge and Lord Chelmsford of the India Office as they believed the destruction of the Ottoman Empire would lead to instability within India itself from its pro-Turkish Muslim population.

Despite opposition, talks with the Arabs over the possibility of a revolt against Istanbul continued through correspondence between Egyptian High Commissioner Sir Henry McMahon and Sharif Hussein. These series of eight letters issued between 14 July 1915 and 30 January 1916, known as the Hussein-McMahon Correspondence, did not constitute an official agreement between Britain and the Arabs over the postwar Middle East. Even so, they represented a diplomatic understanding whereby Britain agreed to the independence of Arabs within not only Arabia, as Kitchener championed, but also Palestine and today's Iraq and Jordan. In addition, the British would recognize Arab independence in Syria east of a line of demarcation that ran through Damascus, Homs, Hama, and Aleppo. Britain refused to grant the Syrian littoral to Hussein, as London asserted that these were areas that did not have a majority Arab population and that France held significant interests there.[12] Hussein acquiesced in this matter but reserved the right to revisit it in the postwar world. In return for these concessions, Hussein would lead an Arab revolt against the Turks and

---

10   Bruce Westrate, *The Arab Bureau: British Policy in the Middle East, 1916-1920* (University Park, PA.: Pennsylvania State University Press, 1992), 14-15.
11   Great Britain, National Archives, War Cabinet Memorandum, "Alexandretta and Mesopotamia", 16 March 1915, CAB 24/1/G.
12   Westrate, 17-19.

enter the war on the side of the Allies. This agreement ultimately led to the 1916 Arab uprising against the Ottoman Empire.

Whilst this agreement infringed on French interests in Syria, the wording in the 14 December 1915 letter left Britain at least some room for diplomatic maneuver. In this letter McMahon asserted that Britain was "free to act without detriment to the interests of her ally, France."[13] Even so, there was clearly a conflict of interest between this agreement and French designs for Syria in the postwar world. This conflict became manifest with an accord struck between the European powers over the partition of the Ottoman Empire upon the conclusion of the war.

This accord was the Sykes-Picot Agreement named after Sir Mark Sykes and Francois Georges Picot, who were the respective representatives of Britain and France. It was the product of French concerns for its territorial goals in the Middle East once Paris became aware of British negotiations between Henry McMahon and Sharif Hussein for Arab entry into the war. Concluded on 16 May 1916, the agreement stipulated that Britain would receive direct control of a portion of Mesopotamia, including Baghdad and Basra, as well as the ports of Haifa and Acre while the majority of Palestine would be internationalized at the conclusion of the war. The British would also establish a sphere of indirect control over the Persian Gulf region, Transjordan, and the rest of Mesopotamia. These territorial claims ensured open lines of communication between Britain and its eastern empire. In return, France would receive direct control over the Syrian littoral west of a line demarcated by the cities of Damascus, Homs, Hama, and Aleppo as well as a portion of southern Anatolia and northern Syria. The remainder of Syria would be under French influence. The Russians, as they too had territorial concerns in the region, would receive territory in the Transcaucasus.[14]

The Sykes-Picot Agreement reflected British goals in the Middle East in the sense that London's primary imperial interest was the oil fields of Mesopotamia, not Palestine or Syria with the exception of the ports of Haifa and Acre that would serve as links to British interests farther east. The agreement also assuaged the fears of France, Britain's principal ally, but it proved to be unworkable from the start. The area promised to France as a zone of French influence was the same one earmarked in the McMahon-Hussein correspondence as a region of independent Arab control in the postwar world. In addition, the Syrian littoral that the agreement promised to France under its direct rule was a region that Hussein viewed as part of Arab lands. While London regarded this agreement as merely upholding pre-existing commitments to France, the contradictions embodied in it were such that most parties in the Middle Eastern theater opposed it. This collection of people became known as

---

13 Westrate, 19.
14 Kenneth Bourne and D. Cameron Watt, eds., *British Documents on Foreign Affairs: Reports and Papers from the Foreign Office Confidential Print*, Part II, Series I, *The Paris Peace Conference of 1919*, Volume 11, *The Turkish Settlement and the Middle East; the Far East*, doc. 14, *"The Sykes-Picot Agreement"*, (Frederick, MD: University Publications of America, 1991), 26-29.

the "Cairo School" (also sometimes referred to as the "Khartoum School") in which many were part of Britain's Arab Bureau. This organization, created in early 1916 and based in Cairo, became Britain's chief intelligence gathering agency in the Middle East. One of its members, David Hogarth, illustrates the misgivings that many had about the Sykes-Picot Agreement. On 3 May 1916, before the signing of the agreements, Hogarth commented that "it cannot but use considerable revision sooner or later for it contains several features which do not promise any final solution to the Near Eastern Question."[15] Rather than implementing the Sykes-Picot Agreement, those in the Cairo School wanted a federation of semi-independent Arab states in the Middle East, particularly in the region of Syria, under British protection. They believed that this course was in Britain's best interests for two reasons. The first was that Syria in the postwar world would be a major transportation center for the entire region in keeping with the railroad construction that had taken place there in the years leading up to the war. In the postwar world as a result, Syria would prove important to British interests farther east. The presence of France, an imperial competitor, in Syria would complicate the use of those assets and thereby threaten British imperial interests in the entire region.[16] Aside from Hogarth, the Cairo School counted Henry McMahon and Director of the Arab Bureau Brigadier General Sir Henry Clayton as principal advocates. The latter individual became the chief political advisor to General Edmund Allenby, the future commander of the Egyptian Expeditionary Force and architect of the Battle of Megiddo. Indeed, Allenby himself became a staunch advocate of the Cairo School as he viewed the Sykes-Picot Agreement as completely unworkable.

The collective implication of these agreements, despite their conflicting nature, necessitated offensives into the Ottoman Empire, including the areas of Palestine and Syria, to lay claim to them pending the end of the war and the partition of the empire. Such offensives would be conducted primarily by the British based in Egypt as they had the majority of Allied forces in the area since the beginning of the war. The prospect of launching any offensives, however, did not at first materialize for numerous reasons. While London crafted agreements with both France and the Arabs on the future of the Middle East, the British remained focused on the strategic goal of defending Egypt and the Suez Canal. Not only were the Ottomans a concern from the east across the Sinai, but a further threat from the west surfaced with the attack of the Senussi, a puritanical sect of Islam, in late 1915 following talks with the Turks supporting such an uprising. While this threat largely vanished after February 1916, the Senussi continued to launch raids against British interests in western Egypt until January 1917 when a final engagement with British forces broke their resolve.

---

15   Westrate, 151.
16   Eyal Zisser, "Britain and the Levant, 1918-1946: A Missed Opportunity?", in Zach Levy and Elie Podeh, eds., *Britain and the Middle East: From Imperial Power to Junior Partner* (Portland, Oregon: Sussex Academic Press, 2008), 139.

In this atmosphere of threats to Egypt and the Suez Canal, the British took steps to try and augment its defenses as the most immediate goal in the theater. Among these steps was the dispatch of Sir Archibald Murray to command British forces in Egypt. Murray, a veteran of the 1888 Zululand Campaign and the 1899-1902 Boer War, began the First World War as a major general and chief of the General Staff of the British Expeditionary Force to France. By September 1915, Murray was chief of the Imperial General Staff before being dismissed in December 1915 by Prime Minister Asquith who believed he was a weak leader. Murray took command of British forces for the defense of eastern Egypt on 9 January 1916, while Lieutenant General Maxwell at first retained command of the defense in western Egypt. This split command structure ultimately proved unworkable, with Murray taking command on 19 March 1916 of all forces within Egypt while simultaneously reorganizing his forces as the Egyptian Expeditionary Force.

Murray's mission was purely a defensive one upon his arrival in Egypt not only as the British perceived a continued threat to the Suez Canal, but it also reflected the grand strategy of the Allies in early 1916. This focused on victory on the Western Front as the means to force Germany and the Central Powers from the war. Championing this Westerner school of thought was Murray's successor as Chief of the Imperial General Staff, General Sir William Robertson. Robertson was a career army officer who had served in India and South Africa. Robertson's orders to Murray were a clear indication of Britain's stance, both in the Middle East and in the war overall: "To keep Egypt reasonably secure. To keep a reserve in Egypt.... To get everybody else to France."[17] As a result of these orders, Murray found his newly constituted Egyptian Expeditionary Force progressively denuded to allow for the manpower requirements of the Western Front.

Finally, offensive operations against the Ottomans in the Near East were hampered by the logistical challenges posed by the diverse and sometimes daunting geography not only in the Sinai, but also in Palestine and Syria in the event that attacks would someday be considered in those regions. The path from Egypt to Aleppo in modern Turkey, that the Egyptian Expeditionary Force ultimately conquered, spans over 500 miles and contains a host of different climates and topographical features. The Sinai Peninsula, that posed the most immediate obstacle to any British advance, was sand desert in the north and mountainous areas in the south while containing no permanent source of running water. Only near the coast was it possible to obtain limited supplies of water by digging 12 to 18 inches underground.[18]

In addition to the problem of the Sinai, the diversity of the topography in Palestine also proved a challenge to the movements of armies. The area of Palestine was smaller than that Wales in the British Isles. The territory stretches only 150 miles from Dan

---

17   David R. Woodward, *Field Marshal Sir William Robertson: Chief of the Imperial General Staff in the Great War* (Westport, Conn.: Praeger, 1998), 116.
18   Archibald Wavell, *The Palestine Campaigns* (London, Constable, 1941), 4.

in the north to Beersheba in the south and 75 miles from the coastal city of Jaffa to the trans-Jordan region of the Hejaz Railroad that ran south through Deraa to points in the Arabian Peninsula. As small as it is, the area encompasses two mountain ranges that run through both Syria and Palestine from north to south and are separated by the Jordan Valley that runs from Lake Tiberias in the north to Aqaba on the coast of the Red Sea. The eastern range, being the mountains of Moab, varied in height from 3,000 to 3,500 feet. The western range of the Judean Hills runs through Jerusalem and averages a height of 2,400 feet.[19] The northern section of the hills, called Samaria, is more open range, but still formidable. In addition to the problems posed for any movements of armies northward over this rough, rocky terrain was the intersection through them of wadis, being dried upriver beds oftentimes sited in deep gorges. Also running north to south through Palestine is the Jordan Valley, which offered no alternative to passage through the mountains as it proved far less hospitable to soldiers owing to so much of it being far below sea level. At Lake Huleh to the north of Lake Tiberias the terrain is only seven feet below sea level, but only ten miles to the south of Lake Tiberias the ground is 680 feet below sea level. The valley in the region of the Dead Sea, only an additional 65 miles to the south of the lake, is 1,300 feet below sea level. As a result, the temperatures average 102 degrees Fahrenheit in an atmosphere where dust storms and swarms of mosquitoes added to the misery of soldiers. An Australian soldier succinctly summed up conditions in the valley when he described it as the "worst and deepest hole in the whole world front."[20] Conditions in the Jordan Valley accounted for a great portion of the cases of malaria suffered by British forces in their eventual drive through the region. In all of Palestine, the only truly hospitable place for troops involved in an advance north was the Plain of Sharon at the coast that stretched from the Mediterranean east for ten to 15 miles before reaching the foothills of the Judean range.

In addition to these varying topographical features running from north to south are two depressions that run from east to west. The first of these is the Plain of Esdraelon in the north that dissects the hilly areas of Galilee in northern Palestine and Samaria to the south. The village of Megiddo that lends its name to Allenby's great 1918 offensive is located at the western entrance of this plain. The second depression runs just north of Jaffa to a point eight miles north of Jericho, which became the area held by the Egyptian Expeditionary Force upon the 1917 conquest of Jerusalem.

Compounding the challenges posed by the varying topographic features of Palestine was, like in the Sinai, the issue of obtaining a sufficient amount of water to supply an army. While there were certainly more constant and plentiful supplies of water available at points in Palestine, such as Jerusalem, this was not enough to launch sustained offensives. It was particularly difficult to water an army in the Judean Hills

---

19 Wavell, 6-7.
20 Edward Woodfin, *Camp and Combat on the Sinai and Palestine Front: The Experience of the British Empire Soldier, 1916-1918* (New York: Palgrave Macmillan, 2012), 128.

during the summer. In that region, rain falls in torrents over a five-month season between November and March. Most of this water, however, runs off quickly in the rocky terrain. This runoff poses a further problem as it turns the region to mud and makes virtually impossible the passage of armies. The problems posed collectively by these topographical features were magnified greatly due to the lack of extensive roads or railway systems. Although dirt track roads transected the region these were mostly impassable during the rainy season. The few metalled roads in Syria and Palestine that existed at the outbreak of war did little to alleviate the problem, particularly in terms of the use of motorized transport.

Finally, a further impediment lay in the fact that the British could do little to offset their logistical problems in a possible offensive through supply from the Mediterranean Sea. Few harbors existed in Syria or Palestine. While small harbors existed at Alexandretta and Beirut in Syria, neither could support large scale logistical operations. Jaffa, farther to the south, posed the same problem because the strong surf and currents on the Mediterranean coast greatly retarded any military landings.[21]

Nevertheless, Murray despite the host of political, military, and logistical considerations that potentially handicapped his situation, endeavored in mid-1916 to conduct limited offensives into the Sinai Peninsula. His aim was the establishment of an active defense, being the creation of forward positions to negate the immediate threat posed to the Suez Canal by the Ottomans. Murray argued that these limited offensives would progressively conquer the Sinai Peninsula and culminate with the capture of el-Arish, a village 30 miles west of the border with Palestine.[22] Once occupied, Murray looked to the establishment of a force capable of striking against any future incursion into the Sinai Peninsula. Chief of the Imperial General Staff Robertson, despite his emphasis on the Western Front, agreed to this plan. He favored the plan in order to prevent future attacks on the Suez Canal, but he also viewed that such a defense would protect manpower reserves within Egypt. The creation of a strategic manpower reserve for possible deployment to the Western Front was one duty assigned to Murray upon his appointment.

The strategic outlook for Murray began to progressively change, however, after 6 December 1916 with the coming to power of David Lloyd George as Prime Minister of Great Britain. Unlike his predecessor, Henry Asquith, the new prime minister favored a different approach to Allied victory that centered, in part, on making the Middle East a major theater of operation. Lloyd George held this view for several reasons. Personally, he held a dislike for the Ottomans, but also he saw achieving victories in the Middle East as part of a wider strategic plan.[23] Lloyd George felt that overall victory rested on close co-operation with all allies on all fronts to collapse the war effort of the Central Powers and he abhorred the central

21   Wavell, 10.
22   John Grainger, *The Battle for Palestine* (Woodbridge, Suffolk: Boydell Press, 2006), 9.
23   Woodward, 55.

focus on the Western Front where operations consumed so many soldiers for so little gain. In his mind, Lloyd George saw a front where all points were equally important and which stretched from Flanders to Switzerland, across the Italian and Balkan fronts to Egypt, and ultimately to Mesopotamia where the front linked up to an eastern section that spread from Persia to the Trans-Caucasus and from the Black Sea to the Baltic Sea.[24] Lloyd George consequently believed that offensives should be carried out along this unified front at points where the enemy was weakest in order to achieve the most gain for the least loss in manpower and material. The Middle East, in his mind, was a particularly enticing theater in this regard. Not only did the new prime minister adhere to this idea militarily, but there was also a political reason for his view. In 1916, Lloyd George wanted to acquire territorial assets from the Central Powers in hopes of using them as leverage at the close of the war to push the Germans from territory that their forces occupied including Belgium, German occupied France, Poland, portions of Romania, Serbia, Montenegro, and Russian territory.[25] In keeping with his overall goal of directing the British war effort on a more global scale, Lloyd George, upon his becoming Prime Minister, created in December 1916 the War Cabinet that comprised five individuals including himself who would direct the war effort.

Lloyd George's belief, expressed through the War Cabinet, became known ultimately as an Easterner point of view. It was one that he had adhered to before becoming prime minister while he was still serving as minister of munitions. As such, the new prime minister was at odds with Chief of Staff General William Robertson, a known Westerner. Secretary to the Committee of Imperial Defense Maurice Hankey commented:

> … at the War Office Lloyd George and Robertson were too different. From the first I realized that would not work together easily, and so it turned out. Lloyd George had never been a partisan of the Western Front policy pursued alone… Consequently the losses on the Somme…were more than he could stand, and during the autumn of 1916 he was becoming daily more disillusioned with his Chief of Staff.[26]

Nevertheless, once Lloyd George became prime minister, Robertson advocated for offensive operations east of the Sinai in an atmosphere where he was generally supportive of progress in the Middle East but did not want operations on a large scale since it held the possibility of siphoning troops away from the Western Front that he believed was the key to victory.

---

24 Maurice Hankey, *The Supreme Command, 1914-1918*, Volume 2 (London: George Allen and Unwin, 1961), 597.
25 Hankey, 599.
26 Hankey, 554.

General Murray, in keeping with the stance of David Lloyd George, believed that an advance into Palestine was possible with the tacit support of Robertson. On 10 December 1916 Murray communicated to Robertson that an advance by the Egyptian Expeditionary Force from Arish in the Sinai Peninsula into Syria was not only possible, but militarily advantageous. Murray advocated the seizure of Raffa in Syria since from there he could strike at Beersheba and thus gain one of the few railway depots in the region. That would leave the Egyptian Expeditionary Force only 70 miles from the Hejaz railway line, which was a major logistical hub for the Ottoman Army in its defense of Syria. Murray believed that from Raffa he could bomb the Hejaz railway with his aircraft and possibly encourage Arab support for the Allied cause against the Turks. This translated into the capture of Raffa on 6 January 1917 in an atmosphere where Robertson was pleased with the operation, but still considered the chief strategic goal of the Egyptian Expeditionary Force to be that of the defense of Egypt rather than large scale advances into Ottoman held territory in keeping with his Westerner point of view: "The West remains the main theater now just as much as it ever did…therefore Palestine remains a secondary theater and must be treated as such."[27]

The projection of the Egyptian Expeditionary Force into Ottoman territory, despite Robertson's estimation of the theatre, provides a fine illustration of Archibald Murray's chief contribution to the Allied war effort in the Middle East and showcases a key reason for the victory of his successor, Edmund Allenby, in the Battle of Megiddo. The success of Murray in his push across the Sinai would not have been possible without his efforts to improve British logistics. In January 1916, the British had already employed 10,000 soldiers and Egyptian laborers to make roads to establish a logistical net spanning the desert of the Sinai and ultimately the rocky hills of Palestine. The roads built by this labor force were used in large part by camels, which the British began procuring even before Murray's tenure. During the first six months of 1915 British Egyptian military authorities had hired through the Egyptian Ministry of the Interior between 1,000 and 1,500 camels and 1,000 Egyptian camel drivers for service in the canal zone between Port Said and the Suez Canal. In the wake of the Turkish assault on the canal, by December 1915 the British created the Camel Transport Corps that consisted of two corps of 10,000 camels each.[28] The value of the Camel Transport Corps, and camels in general until the corps was dissolved in early 1917 in favor of motorized transport, cannot be overestimated because the organization served as the core of British logistical support against the Ottomans in the Sinai and Palestine. Between December 1915 and December 1918 the number of men involved in the camel service averaged 25,000 in an atmosphere where the war

27 Sir William Robertson to Lord Milne, 8 May 1917, in David R. Woodward, ed. *The Military Correspondence of Field Marshal Sir William Robertson, Chief of the Imperial General Staff, December 1915-February 1918* (London: Bodley Head, 1989), 184.
28 G.E. Badcock, *A History of the Transport Services of the Egyptian Expeditionary Force, 1916-1917-1918* (London: Hugh Rees, 1925), 20.

claimed many of their lives. By the war's conclusion, the corps suffered 163 killed and 1,458 wounded in combat, 4,010 dead from disease, 78 missing in action, and 66 lost as prisoners of war.[29] The members of this force endured not only the hardships of combat, but also the rigors of the harsh terrain through which a camel company could average about 15 miles per day at a pace of 2.5 miles per hour. By early 1917, the corps' main base was at Kantara. Known as Number 1 Depot, Kantara not only supported the camel corps, but also the horses of the Egyptian Expeditionary Force's cavalry. As such, Kantara was one of the largest horse depots in the world with care provided for 8,000 horses. It remained the main supply depot for the Egyptian Expeditionary Force's livestock throughout the war.

In addition, Kantara also served as the water supply for the Egyptian Expeditionary Force's offensives into Palestine, including the Battle of Megiddo, and ultimately the subsequent drive into Syria. By July 1917, water was mostly obtained directly from the Nile River through the Sweet Water Canal at Kantara. The plant at Kantara filtered some 600,000 gallons of water per diem through twelve-inch, ten-inch, and eight-inch steel pipes. Smaller lines then stretched south of Beersheba by the end of the war. The rather dirty water of the Nile passed through a plant comprised of strainers made of brass wire gauze before being pumped to a settling tank where sediments from the water were filtered for 10 hours. Finally, the water passed through a filter containing sand before being mixed with chloride of lime. The process removed 95 percent of harmful bacteria and organisms.[30] This supply proved absolutely vital to Murray and ultimately Allenby in the Battle of Megiddo as the western Sinai had only a few wells capable of supporting a limited number of troops, but not an army. The eastern portion of the Sinai proved still more daunting to supply as it was practically waterless. The center at Kantara was critical to an army whose water allotment for a cavalry division amounted to 120,000 gallons daily while an infantry division consumed 60,000 gallons in the same space of time.[31] Camels were then used to transport the water past the terminuses of the pipeline to British forces in the field. By the end of the war, the water supply system for the Egyptian Expeditionary Force comprised 147 miles of pipeline from the filter plant at Kantara to points east and 220 miles from the Nile River.[32] In terms of logistics, Archibald Murray was in large part responsible for British success in the Near East during the First World War. Indeed, Allenby himself recognized Murray's contribution in a dispatch on 28 June 1919:

> I desire to express my indebtedness to my predecessor, Lieutenant General Sir A.J. Murray, who, by his bridging the desert between Egypt and Palestine, laid

---

29   Badcock, 30.
30   R.J.S. McDowall, "The Water Supply of the Egyptian Expeditionary Force, with Special Reference to the Efficiency of Mechanical Rapid Filtration with Chlorination", *The Journal of Hygiene*, Vol. 19, No. 3 (January 1921), 306-307.
31   Great Britain, National Archives, War Office Directorate, WO 106/614, 4.
32   McDowall, 308.

the foundation of the subsequent advances of the Egyptian Expeditionary Force. I reaped the fruits of his foresight and strategical imagination, which brought the waters of the Nile to the borders of Palestine...The organization he created, both in Sinai and in Egypt, stood all tests and formed the cornerstone of my successes.[33]

Given this estimation, Murray stands as one of the more successful generals for the British in theaters outside of the European Western Front.

Even so, Murray is known less for his logistical achievements and more for the events that ultimately led to his removal from command of the Egyptian Expeditionary Force. The genesis of Murray's downfall was the result of problems incurred in his drive east due to a situation born from Robertson's emphasis on the Western Front over all else in the months leading up to the accession of Lloyd George as prime minister. By the end of the first quarter of 1916, Robertson had taken 10 divisions from Murray's command in the belief that the Turks could deploy no more than 100,000 soldiers in an operation against the Suez Canal. This left Murray with a denuded infantry of four divisions supplemented by British Yeomanry, the Australian Light Horse, and the New Zealand Mounted Rifles.[34] With this force Murray intended to attack Turkish positions along a defensive line that ran between Gaza and Beersheba in Palestine. This line was crucial to the Turkish defense of Jerusalem farther north.

While the British still held a preponderance of force over the Turks, their numbers proved unable to conquer the city of Gaza, being a lynchpin in the Turkish defensive line. Battles there proved to be the end for Murray as commander of the Egyptian Expeditionary Force. Despite the reduction of soldiers, the British fielded 11,000 cavalry earmarked to surround Gaza and thereby block possible Turkish reinforcement of the city. Additionally, a force of 12,000 rifles had orders to push into Gaza. The Battle of First Gaza unfolded on 26-27 March 1917 and proved a great disappointment for the British. Not only did the city hold, but the British suffered 523 dead and 4,000 casualties overall.[35] Murray's dispatch to London concerning First Gaza proved a colossal mistake for the general. Rather than portraying it as a strategic setback, the general cast the operation as victory:

> On the 26th and 27th we were heavily engaged in this neighborhood with a force of about 20,000 of the enemy. We inflicted very heavy losses on him and have taken 900 prisoners, including GOC and whole divisional staff of the Fifty-Third Turkish Division...The operation was most successful, and owing to the fog and waterless nature of the country round Gaza just fell short of a complete disaster to the enemy ...[36]

---

33 Cyril Falls, *Armageddon 1918* (London: Weidenfeld and Nicolson, 1964), 20.
34 Archibald P. Wavell, *The Palestine Campaigns* (London: Constable, 1928), 92.
35 Woodward, 65.
36 O. Teichman, *The Diary of a Yeomanry M.O.* (London: T. Fisher and Unwin, 1921), 124-125.

In truth, the British faced only 4,000 Turkish troops and inflicted 2,447 losses in a battle where the British offensive bogged down in the face of a well-entrenched enemy force. A second battle to take Gaza between 17-19 April 1917 was a more resounding defeat for the British in large part due to Turkish reinforcement of the area. In the Second Battle of Gaza the British suffered 6,444 casualties as opposed to 2,013 Ottoman.[37] Despite Murray's initial assessment it was quite evident to London that the British offensive in the Near East against the Ottoman Empire had stalled.

The reaction of the government to Murray's performance was not only fast, but underway even before the Second Battle of Gaza. A meeting of the War Cabinet on 6 April 1917 centered solely on the subject of whether Murray was fit for command. The conclusion of the cabinet was a telling one in terms of the doubts expressed about the general of the Egyptian Expeditionary Force:

> General Sir Archibald Murray should retain the command, at any rate, until the forthcoming operation has taken place. In the meantime, the Chief of the Imperial General Staff was instructed to consider who would be the most suitable successor in order that the question might be re-examined by the War Cabinet, if necessary, after the battle [Second Gaza].[38]

The cabinet reached this conclusion primarily due to Chief of the Imperial General Staff Robertson's assertion that installing a new commander on the eve of the Second Battle of Gaza would stall operations that were already in the planning stage. Prime Minister Lloyd George's musings on the situation after Second Gaza, however, were even more blunt: "The Palestine campaign ... had been conducted with a flabbiness and lack of nerve which presented a wretched contrast to the dash and resolution ... in Mesopotamia."[39] Clearly, Murray's tenure was over in the wake of the first two battles of Gaza.

In keeping with the directive from the 6 April 1917 War Cabinet meeting, Robertson ultimately proposed the appointment of Lieutenant General Edmund Allenby as an individual who could reinvigorate the sagging British effort in the Near East. Born in 1861, Allenby graduated in 1882 from the Royal Military College at Sandhurst as a cavalry officer. A descendant of Oliver Cromwell, he exhibited traits in his pre-1914 career that served him well as commander of the Egyptian Expeditionary Force. He served in the 1899-1902 Boer War where he learned to appreciate giving his trusted subordinates wide latitude to achieve objectives rather than relying on a strict

---

37 For numbers on both First and Second Gaza, see Spencer C. Tucker, ed., *The Encyclopedia of World War I: A Political, Social, and Military History*, Volume 2 (Santa Barbara, CA.: ABC-CLIO, 2005), 467-468.
38 Great Britain, National Archives, *Minutes and Conclusions of the War Cabinet*, CAB 24/44B, "Palestine, the Chief Military Command, 6 April 1917, 5.
39 David Lloyd George, *The War Memoirs of David Lloyd George*, Volume 6, *1918* (Boston: Little, Brown, 1937), 201.

command structure. He also was a believer in combined arms tactics as Inspector General of the Cavalry, a position he held by 1910. He strove to wed the destructive firepower of the machine gun to the shock power of cavalry. While the tall, heavy, Allenby did tend towards an explosive temper, earning him the nickname "The Bull", he entered the Fist World War with a reputation as a capable commander.[40]

Despite this pre-war assessment, Allenby arrived in Cairo, Egypt on 27 June 1917 in an environment where the general saw his appointment as being a demotion based on his performance on the Western Front. In his prior capacity Allenby commanded the Third Army in the 9-24 April 1917 Second Battle of Arras under British Expeditionary Force commander Field Marshal Sir Douglas Haig. Allenby had planned to take advantage of a network of cellars under the town of Arras that could hold upwards of 20,000 troops to avoid German reconnaissance aircraft and artillery barrage. Haig, however, shelved Allenby's plan in favor of a conventional attack preceded by a five hour artillery barrage.[41] Allenby blundered in the ensuing operation as he chose a massed attack against German positions rather than a series of small scale infantry attacks advocated by Haig. The consequent failure of the operation as a whole led to Allenby being relieved of his command. Indeed, on news of his replacement Allenby broke down.[42] By the time that he left France for Egypt, Allenby believed that he had been exiled to a theater of little importance to the overall Allied war effort.

Nonetheless, Allenby's leadership style brought a transformation in the Egyptian Expeditionary Force whose morale was quite low from the failures of Murray at Gaza. Allenby proved to be a much more hands-on commander than Murray, making his first inspection of British defenses in the region of Beersheba on 4 June 1917 only days after his arrival in the theater. Indeed, one British soldier claimed that within 48 hours of his arrival Allenby had already made the acquaintance of every officer in every branch of his general headquarters.[43] Such contact made a lasting impression and had a direct effect on morale. Allenby proved much more capable at communicating with those around him than the aloof Murray:

> I cannot adequately describe the far reaching effect this simple act had on all such small fry as myself; you felt instinctively like there was nothing you would not try your best to do, and from the date of his arrival as our Commander-in-Chief a totally different atmosphere permeated our whole existence…He went everywhere, saw everything, and possessed moreover that faculty as wonderful as it is rare of always remembering everyone he had met.[44]

---

40 Falls, 26-28.
41 Lawrence James, *Imperial Warrior: The Life and Times of Field-Marshal Viscount Allenby,1861-1936* (London: Weidenfeld and Nicolson, 1993), 95.
42 James, 107.
43 O. Teichman, *The Diary of a Yeomanry M.O* (London: T. Fisher and Unwin, 1921), 162-163.
44 Badcock, 316.

This feeling serves as a reflection of Allenby's tendency to rely heavily on those around him for success as he proved to be a delegator that surrounded himself with people he thought most capable of accomplishing his goals. Historian Brian Gardner, in his Allenby biography, asserted that a key reason for Allenby's hands on approach was that the general was a good administrator but did not have a very agile mind. In the words of T.E. Lawrence when commenting on Allenby, 'His Mind was like the prow of the *Mauretania*. There is so much weight behind it that it does not need to be sharp as a razor.'[45] While this assessment may not be overly complimentary of the general, it is not an indictment of his leadership abilities. Rather, it is a testimony to a good leader who, in the Battle of Megiddo, provided direction to his officers after which he maintained confidence in their judgement as a means of success.

Whilst Allenby became familiar with his new command and began to contemplate a resumption of offensive operations in Palestine, he faced a newly reorganized Ottoman defense of Palestine and Syria. Since the opening of 1917, the Ottomans focused on reconstituting their military forces in the wake of setbacks not only in the Sinai against the Suez Canal and the consequent push of the British towards Gaza, but also in Mesopotamia. The Ottoman high command looked to operations to seize the strategic initiative in both theaters from the allies. This drive was in part the result of successful campaigns in the Balkans as well as the strengthening of the Ottoman war effort through German and Austrian assistance. As a result, Minister of War Enver Pasha called for the creation of a new army group that would first be deployed to Palestine to push the British back towards the Suez Canal before being re-deployed east to retake Baghdad, Mesopotamia, and Persia from Allied forces. The Ottomans named this new group the Yildirim, or Thunderbolt, Army Group.[46] This force consisted at its core of the Ottoman 6th and 7th armies and was distinctly an organization of both Turkish and German composition. The German high command referred to Yildirim as Army Group F in an atmosphere where Germany clearly held a great deal of influence over the command of the group. The Yildirim staff on its inception consisted of only nine Turkish officers whereas there were 65 German officers. German troops provided to the new group, however, did not reflect the preponderance of Germans on the staff. Attached to Yildirim was only the German Asia Corps. Essentially a brigade, this force included an artillery battalion, a squadron of aircraft, and motorized transport.[47]

Operational planning for this new army group proved a source of great contention within the Ottoman High Command and lasted through much of 1917. At first, the Ottoman High Command on 24 June 1917 contemplated using Yildirim Army Group to retake Baghdad. Only in September 1917 was this plan abandoned in favor

---

45 Brian Gardner, *Allenby of Arabia: Lawrence's General* (New York: Coward-McCann, 1965), 203.
46 Erickson, 160.
47 Erickson, 169.

of the deployment of Yildirim to Palestine under the command of General Erich von Falkenhayn.[48] This decision was the result of reports from Kress von Kressenstein, in command of defenses in Palestine, that the British were undertaking massive logistical preparations for a renewed offensive along the Gaza-Beersheba line.

Ottoman intelligence reports proved correct that the British were planning a major offensive in Palestine with the object of seizing Jerusalem. Following a meeting in London on 7 July 1917 between Allenby, Lloyd George, and Robertson, the prime minister stated that he wanted Jerusalem taken before Christmas. British intelligence reports led them to believe that the Ottoman defense lay across a 30-mile line that extended from Gaza to Beersheba in which the Turks fielded five infantry divisions and one cavalry division comprised of 46,000 rifles, 2,600 sabers being cavalry, 200 artillery pieces, and 250 machine guns.[49] Allenby planned for an attack against Gaza as a feint for his primary objective of Beersheba in order to secure that area's water wells. Such a plan, however, met with a degree of opposition within the War Cabinet as Allenby requested reinforcement of his army for a push towards Jerusalem. In his mind, the Ottomans would do all in their power to prevent the fall of Jerusalem, meaning that his Egyptian Expeditionary Force needed greater force strength versus possible Turkish reinforcement. Allenby estimated that he required a force consisting of seven infantry divisions and three cavalry divisions. Robertson, in a War Cabinet meeting on 10 August 1917, laid out his case against such a move in keeping with his Westerner point of view. He reasoned that Allenby's requirements were perhaps necessary given the end of Russian operations in the Caucasus region and the shift of Turkish efforts to the defense of Palestine. Even so, the manpower requirements given that fact were far greater than could be supplied due to the possibility that Russia might withdraw completely from the war. If that situation occurred, Robertson pointed out that the Western Front would require every last available soldier because the Central Powers would shift all of their military assets west. Rather than a massive drive towards Jerusalem, Robertson advocated the provision of one extra division and artillery from Salonica by November in order to allow Allenby to press the Turks in support of British operations in Persia. These offensives in the general's mind might still take Jerusalem, but with far fewer forces strength than those requested by Allenby.[50] The War Cabinet agreed with Robertson's assessment. Allenby in correspondence with Robertson shortly thereafter recognized London's desire to slow operations in his theater when he wrote "The War Cabinet's instructions are sufficient and clear…I feel that I understand exactly.[51]

The exchange in August 1917, however, was merely the beginning rather than the end of the debate over the commitment of resources to the Palestinian theater as the

---

48   Erickson, 171.
49   Hankey, 685.
50   Great Britain, National Archives, *Report of Cabinet Committee on War Policy*, CAB 24/4/G179, 10 August 1917, 32-34.
51   Woodward, *Field Marshal Sir William Robertson*, 159.

argument between the Western and Eastern strategic schools of thought continued. This debate rested on Russia's declining military fortunes and Allenby's belief that as a result he would face far more Turkish strength as he drove north. While Allenby's Egyptian Expeditionary Force managed to secure the Gaza-Beersheba line by 14 November 1917, the general believed that he would face almost the entire strength of the Turkish army in a push towards Jerusalem that would see his forces arrayed on a line between Jaffa and Jerusalem. In this context, Allenby asserted that he required an additional 13 divisions for a push towards Jerusalem.[52] Such a reinforcement was absolutely impossible given the requirements of the Western Front and was refused outright by the War Cabinet. Robertson asserted that the current force strength of Allenby's command was sufficient to win Jerusalem, but not pursue operations north of the Jaffa to Jerusalem line. The simmering disagreement between Allenby and Robertson, and the latter's ulterior motive of limiting operations in the Middle East on the argument of force requirements, was turned on its head when the Egyptian Expeditionary Force captured Jerusalem on 9 December 1917. This achievement laid bare a clear intelligence gap in terms of the British assessment of Turkish military strength in Palestine. In the wake of the fall of Jerusalem British intelligence revealed that the Turks fielded only 21,000 troops in all of Palestine while Robertson maintained that the number stood at 120,000.[53] In this context Robertson faced increasing pressure from David Lloyd George as to future operations in Palestine since the prime minister desired further eastern efforts against the Turks.

This situation led to a reassessment of the Allied war effort in Palestine that ultimately produced the Battle of Megiddo. With pressure mounting against his resistance to a larger campaign against the Ottomans in Palestine, Robertson wrote to Allenby that the members of the War Cabinet wished to know the feasibility of not only continuing offensive operations aimed at seizing all of Palestine, but also whether it was possible to advance through Palestine and Syria to Aleppo.[54] This request produced a proposal in late January 1918 concerning future operations against the Ottomans. This was the culmination of the debate between Lloyd George and Robertson over the focus of Allied resources against the Central Powers. The proposal originated from the new Supreme War Council, being an attempt to consolidate Allied resources for best use to achieve victory against the Central Powers. Established in November 1917, the organization met in late January 1918 and advocated a defensive stance on the Western Front, given the reversals in that theater during 1917. It focused on peripheral theaters in keeping with Lloyd George's Eastern school of thought. The Permanent Military Representatives of the council believed that the Allies should "undertake a decisive operation against Turkey with a view to the annihilation of the

---

52 Woodward, 162.
53 Woodward, 163.
54 Great Britain, National Archives, *Future Operations in Palestine, Appendix III*, CAB 24/37, 14 December 1917, 33.

Turkish armies and the collapse of Turkish resistance."[55] Robertson maintained that such an offensive was not possible given the situation on the Western Front where any diminution of force strength would threaten Allied fortunes in that theater. In a letter to Field Marshal Douglas Haig, commander-in-chief of the British Expeditionary Force, on 24 January 1918 Robertson in no uncertain terms stated his steadfast opposition to the expansion of the war effort in Palestine: "I find that Versailles (Supreme War Council) have just sent in a paper advocating an offensive…to knock out the Turk. The paper is damned rot in general."[56] Robertson had a powerful ally for his point of view. French Premier Georges Clemenceau trusted Robertson's assessment that an expansion of operations in the east would be dangerous to the Allied prospects of winning the war on the Western Front.[57] As a result Lloyd George felt compelled to promise no more troops to Palestine despite the recommendation of the Supreme War Council. Reinforcing the decision of the Prime Minister in the months that followed was the 21 March 1918 opening of the Ludendorff Offensive, which was the last major German offensive on the Western Front.

Robertson's victory over Lloyd George proved short-lived in terms of the general's career as commander in chief of the Imperial General Staff. On 18 February 1918 Lloyd George removed Robertson over not only the Palestinian question, but also disagreement over the amount of control that the inter-allied Supreme War Council should have over British military decisions. His replacement, Field Marshal Sir Henry Wilson, proved more supportive of Lloyd George's Easterner view. As the British representative to the Supreme War Council in the months prior to his appointment as chief of the Imperial General Staff, Wilson exhibited a good ability to liaise with Allied representatives as part of the increasing drive towards unity of command for the Allies. Even so, despite Wilson's more receptive view to a renewed drive in Palestine he felt compelled to advocate the Western Front as the primary allied theater given the massive scale of the German spring offensive. Lloyd George consequently labelled him "Wully (Robertson) redivivius."[58]

The renewed emphasis on the Western Front served only to reinforce a situation in Palestine where Allenby, despite his success in taking Jerusalem, could not advance farther. This situation was in large part not the result of a lack of manpower, but of logistical support north of Jerusalem. Two assaults east into the Jordan River Valley in order to disrupt Turkish efforts against Allenby's right flank only produced halting success. The attack against Amman between 21 March and 2 April 1918 failed in large part because of terrain as Amman, some 30 miles from Jericho as the crow flies, is an area covered by scrub brush and intersected by wadis. Also, the terrain proved difficult to traverse since for the first five miles from Jericho British forces

55 Hankey, 767.
56 Sir William Robertson to Field Marshal Sir Douglas Haig, 24 January 1918, in David R. Woodward, ed. *The Military Correspondence of Field Marshal Sir William Robertson*, 274.
57 Woodward, *Field Marshal Sir William Robertson*, 166.
58 Woodward, 168.

advanced over terrain that rose only 500 feet, but over the next 12 miles the terrain rose in altitude another 3,500 feet to the plateau of Moab. Finally, torrential rains greatly hampered the operation.[59] A further attack on Es Salt between 30 April-4 May resulted in limited success, but the British were not able to hold the area.

The reason for the failure to hold Es Salt reflected a growing problem for Allenby that greatly retarded further advances by the Egyptian Expeditionary Force. On 5 June 1918 Allenby wrote to Wilson and stated "I cannot, at my present strength, maintain troops in the mountains of E. of Jordan … I am not strong enough to make holding attacks … and the Turks can transfer their reserves … as required."[60] Allenby's statement stemmed from a process already underway where, given the manpower requirements on the Western Front to counter the massive German offensive, led to the redeployment of many of the Egyptian Expeditionary Force's units to France at the same time as the operations in the Jordan River Valley.

This signaled a reorganization of Allenby's command where the loss of troops was progressively bridged through the introduction of more imperial troops, specifically Indians, to the Egyptian Expeditionary Force. This process did not start with the outbreak of the Ludendorff Offensive. Historian Kaushik Roy commented in his work on the Indian army that "The crisis of March 1918 did not begin the process of Indianization but did alter the rate at which it was enacted."[61] Robertson in late 1917, while still Chief of the Imperial General Staff, advocated for the plan of action in order to prevent the loss of troops from the Western Front. The deliberation of the War Cabinet on 27 March 1918 greatly accelerated the process of Indianization as Allenby faced the redeployment of his troops coupled with the introduction of further Indian units: "General Allenby ought to be warned to prepare for a reduction in his strength. General Wilson stated that Allenby had under his command three Divisions of white troops, of which two should be temporarily withdrawn…to facilitate embarkation to France if required."[62] The War Cabinet promptly approved the course of action in the same meeting. As a result of this move, the Egyptian Expeditionary Force that had conquered Jerusalem was virtually dismantled through redirection of troops to the Western Front. Indeed, on the same date as the meeting of the War Cabinet the War Office sent a cable to Allenby for him to adopt an active defense of Palestine rather than pursue any more offensive operations.[63] By the time the process

---

59 H. Pirie Gordon, *A Brief Record of the Advance of the Egyptian Expeditionary Force* (London, HMSO: 1919), 18.
60 Edmund Allenby to Sir Henry Wilson, 5 June 1918, in Matthew Hughes, *Allenby in Palestine: The Middle East Correspondence of Field Marshal Viscount Allenby, June 1917-October 1919* (Stroud: Sutton Publishing, 2004), 160.
61 Kaushik Roy, ed. *The Indian Army in the Two World Wars* (Boston, MA: Brill, 2012), 175.
62 Great Britain, National Archives, *Minutes and Conclusions of the War Cabinet*, CAB 23/14, 27 March 1918, 2.
63 War Office to Edmund Allenby, 27 March 1918, in Matthew Hughes, *Allenby in Palestine*, 138.

of reorganization was over, Allenby's command ultimately lost two full divisions, over 30 infantry battalions, and a dozen regiments of cavalry. This left the Egyptian Expeditionary Force before reinforcements of Indian troops with one complete division, three greatly denuded divisions, and two cavalry divisions. All told, Allenby lost over 60,000 seasoned troops to the requirements of the Ludendorff Offensive.[64] No further offensives were possible given this state of affairs until new units could be trained thus prepared for combat.

The force Allenby ultimately produced through efforts to reorganize his army created the Egyptian Expeditionary Force that triumphed over the Turks in the Battle of Megiddo. The reorganization of the Desert Mounted Corps, the cavalry of the Egyptian Expeditionary Force, under the command of Major General Sir Henry Chauvel, proved to be the less difficult task. The Indian cavalry forces earmarked for Allenby's command came from the Western Front and thus were already well trained. In addition, Major-General Sir G. de S. Barrow and Major-General H.J.M. Macandrew of the Desert Mounted Corps both had prior experience with Indian cavalry. These generals respectively commanded the 4th and 5th Cavalry Divisions of the corps that were the majority of the Desert Mounted Corps' force strength. Within each of the three brigades in these divisions were a regiment of British yeomanry and two of Indian cavalry. The only exception proved the 15th brigade of the 5th Cavalry Division that consisted of Jodhpur, Mysore, and Hyderabad Lancers.[65] The remainder of the corps consisted of the Australian Mounted Division under the command of Major-General H.W. Hodgson with three brigades.

The reorganization of the infantry proved a more daunting task than that of the cavalry. The first replacement Indian troops began to arrive in theater during February, but the process lasted until August in an atmosphere where the troops arrived in a series of small numbers at a time. Some of these soldiers were well trained and had battle experience as battalions of Indian infantry from Egypt and Mesopotamia constituted part of their number. Even so, Allenby recognized a potential danger with the use of these forces against the Ottomans as ultimately 29% of the new infantry were Muslim, which raised fears that many would desert to the Muslim Ottomans in time of combat.[66] In addition, many of the new recruits were completely untrained. An attempt to offset potential problems of command and control was a scheme whereby each of the seven infantry divisions of the reconstituted Egyptian Expeditionary Force would consist of three British and nine Indian battalions. Still, Allenby had grave reservations about the efficacy of his force in terms of training. Matters came to a head

---

64   David Bullock, *Allenby's War: The Palestine-Arabian Campaigns, 1916-1918* (London: Blandford Press, 1988), 113.
65   Cyril Falls, *History of the Great War, based on Official Documents, Military Operations Egypt and Palestine, 1914-1918*, Volume II, *From June 1917 to the End of the War* (London: HMSO, 1930), 415-417.
66   James E. Kitchen, "The Indianization of the Egyptian Expeditionary Force: Palestine 1918" in Kaushik Roy, ed. *The Indian Army in the Two World Wars*, 174-175.

with the 54th Division that remained wholly British when the War Office tried in June 1918 to redeploy it to the Western Front. This event was the only time that Allenby protested over the reorganization of his force in keeping with the fear that many of his new Indian troops were not trained and thus his force would be vulnerable to attack:

> Of the 54 Battalions [of Indian troops] 22 have proved their value in war…10 battalions, though composed of men who have seen service, are newly formed units, and the remaining 22 have seen no service and are in varying stages of training. The recruits, of whom there are a large number, have, in some cases, not even fired a musketry course. On the whole I am bound to say that I consider that it will be some months before the last 22 battalions can be considered thoroughly reliable, and to take away more British or Colonial troops involves a serious risk. too few British troops in the force might prove a problem for command and control.[67]

Lloyd George shared Allenby's concerns on two counts. Not only did he believe that the lack of training was a problem and this might thereby threaten Allenby's efforts to hold Jerusalem, but he also distrusted Indian troops on the whole for the same religious reasons held by Allenby.[68]

While the fears of desertion on religious grounds ultimately proved unfounded, the concerns about training were quite justified and extended beyond the lack of rifle training. Part of the problem in terms of the lack of military training was a practice put into place in British Imperial India in the wake of the 1857 Sepoy Mutiny where British officials organized Indian battalions on the basis of ethnic, religious, economic, and even geographical grounds in an attempt to foster a degree of cohesion. Oftentimes, military effectiveness was a secondary consideration. In addition, there was a basic logistical problem in Indian units as rations for Muslim troops and Hindu troops varied on religious grounds. That was only one aspect of a wider problem where the British needed an understanding of the cultural norms of their men. The British and Indian troops alike also had to overcome a language barrier. Indeed, in one battalion of the newly formed force there were only two British officers who could understand their new recruits while only one Indian officer spoke English.[69] Allenby instituted programs beginning in June 1918 to address both the problems of different cultural norms and the language barrier. By the eve of the Battle of Megiddo the British maintained examinations for officers to learn Indian customs and Hindustani, as this was the language of the majority of Indian troops.[70]

---

67 Great Britain, National Archives, Allenby to War Office, 15 June 1918, CAB 24/54, 2.
68 Great Britain, National Archives, Notes on the meeting with the Prime Minister, 26 June 1918, CAB 23/44A, 2.
69 Cyril Falls, *History of the Great War, based on Official Documents, Military Operations Egypt and Palestine, 1914-1918*, Volume II, *From June 1917 to the End of the War*, 418-419.
70 Great Britain, National Archives, British Army War Diaries, 3 September 1918, WO 95/4704, 14-15.

All told, the reorganization of the Egyptian Expeditionary Force was a daunting endeavor that unfolded rapidly over the space of largely six months. The force that emerged from the process was stronger in some respects while lacking in others. In terms of cavalry, Allenby found himself in a better position than before the reorganization. The Desert Mounted Corps had three divisions armed with saber and lances as shock troops while the fourth, the Australian and New Zealand Mounted Division, was under separate command and comprised mounted rifles. British officers commanded most of the brigades in these divisions with some exceptions being the Indian brigades drawn from the princely states of the British Raj such as the Mysore, Hyderabad, and Jodhpur Lancers. The infantry, on the other hand, while having newly reconstituted divisions that would serve with distinction, were definitely not as combat efficient as those that Allenby commanded prior to the process of reorganization. An example of this concerns the 60th Division that, when transferred to the Mediterranean coast for operations in the Battle of Megiddo, exhibited problems with the command and control of Indian troops.[71] Doubts also remained over the religious question, which the Turks themselves saw as an opportunity. As reorganization progressed Turkish frontline patrols brought their regimental imams to sing holy greetings and prayers to the British forces in hopes of sparking mass desertions of Indian Muslims to their ranks.[72] In truth, these practices had only halting success. From April 1918 until the end of the war only 30 Indian soldiers deserted amidst British suspicions that they had gone to the enemy.[73] Even so, Allenby took steps throughout the remainder of British operations in the Near Middle East to guard against this potential threat. On 9 September, ten days before the Battle of Megiddo, Allenby issued express orders to his corps commanders to tell no Indian troops of impending operations until absolutely necessary.[74] While much progress had been made, the Egyptian Expeditionary Force did have perceived weaknesses in the minds of its commander and his subordinates.

Despite its problems, the Egyptian Expeditionary Force emerged from reorganization as a capable fighting force supplemented by both air and mechanized ground units. In the former category Allenby had at his disposal the Palestinian Brigade of the Royal Air Force under the command of Brigadier General A.E. Borton that had two wings of seven squadrons. Within these were Bristol fighter planes, SE5 fighters, and one Handley Page bomber. In the latter arena Allenby had two light armored

---

71 Great Britain, Imperial War Museum, ES Powell MSS, PP/MCR/37, 133.
72 James E. Kitchen, "The Indianization of the Egyptian Expeditionary Force: Palestine 1918", in Kaushik Roy, ed. *The Indian Army in the Two World Wars*, 175.
73 Great Britain, British Library, Oriental and India Office Collections, "Nominal Rolls of Indian Prisoners of War, Suspected of Having Deserted to the Enemy or of Having Given Information to or Otherwise Assisted the Enemy After Capture: Egyptian Expeditionary Force", L/MIL/17/5/2403, 2-3.
74 Great Britain, National Archives, War Diaries of the GHQ Egyptian Expeditionary Force, Allenby to Corps Commanders, 9 September, 1918, WO 95/4371.

car batteries and two light car patrol batteries. These supplemented one of the most culturally and ethnically diverse commands of 1914-18. The Egyptian Expeditionary Force was anything but a British Army. It was an imperial, Allied army comprised of troops from Britain, Australia, New Zealand, India, Hong Kong, Singapore, France, Italy, South Africa, and Egypt. It also had a Jewish contingent with the 38th, 39th, and 40th Royal Fusiliers in keeping with the goal of Zionism to found a Jewish state in the region of Palestine after the war. It was this mixed army that won one of the greatest victories of the First World War – The Battle of Megiddo.

3

Planning and Preparations

The reorganization of the Egyptian Expeditionary Force occurred during a period of little offensive operations by the British in the Palestinian theater in the months leading up to September 1918. Not only was this due to the process of training new troops in general, it was also the result of the fact that the time between May to August 1918 were the peak summer months in the region. The extreme heat was a problem for men experiencing combat, but this also directly affected the logistical support of the army. The coastal area of the British defensive line extending from Jerusalem to Jaffa registered 80 degrees Fahrenheit whilst the eastern portion of the front, in the Jordan River Valley, averaged 120 degrees Fahrenheit due to its being below sea level. In both sectors troops had to contend with disease in the form of malaria fostered by the mosquitos that thrived at the height of summer.[1] The combination of these two issues ensured no new British offensive operation of any size would occur.

In this situation Allenby fully recognized that the key to extended operations past the Jerusalem-Jaffa line lay with the extension of the logistical net. These efforts occurred throughout 1918 and by the opening of the Battle of Megiddo the British found themselves in a very good position. Among the efforts used to accomplish this end was an extension of the British railway line. By the summer of 1918 the railway line could transport some 2,000 tons of goods and equipment a day to the front. Supplementing this was a relocation of the main supply depot of the Egyptian Expeditionary Force to a point closer to Allenby's army. In April 1918 the main wheat center was moved from the Sinai Peninsula to what became known as No. 2 Depot at Bir Salem near Ludd.[2] Complementing the wheat depot was the entry point for supplies into Port Said in Egypt. This center could hold 4,500 tons of meat and also housed a bakery. All told, rations for the Egyptian Expeditionary Force proved sufficient in the months leading

---

1   Cyril Falls, *History of the Great War, based on Official Documents, Military Operations Egypt and Palestine, 1914-1918*. Volume II. *From June 1917 to the End of the War* (London: HMSO, 1930), 422-423.
2   G.E. Badcock, *A History of the Transport Services of the Egyptian Expeditionary Force, 1916-1917-1918* (London: Hugh Rees, 1925), 23.

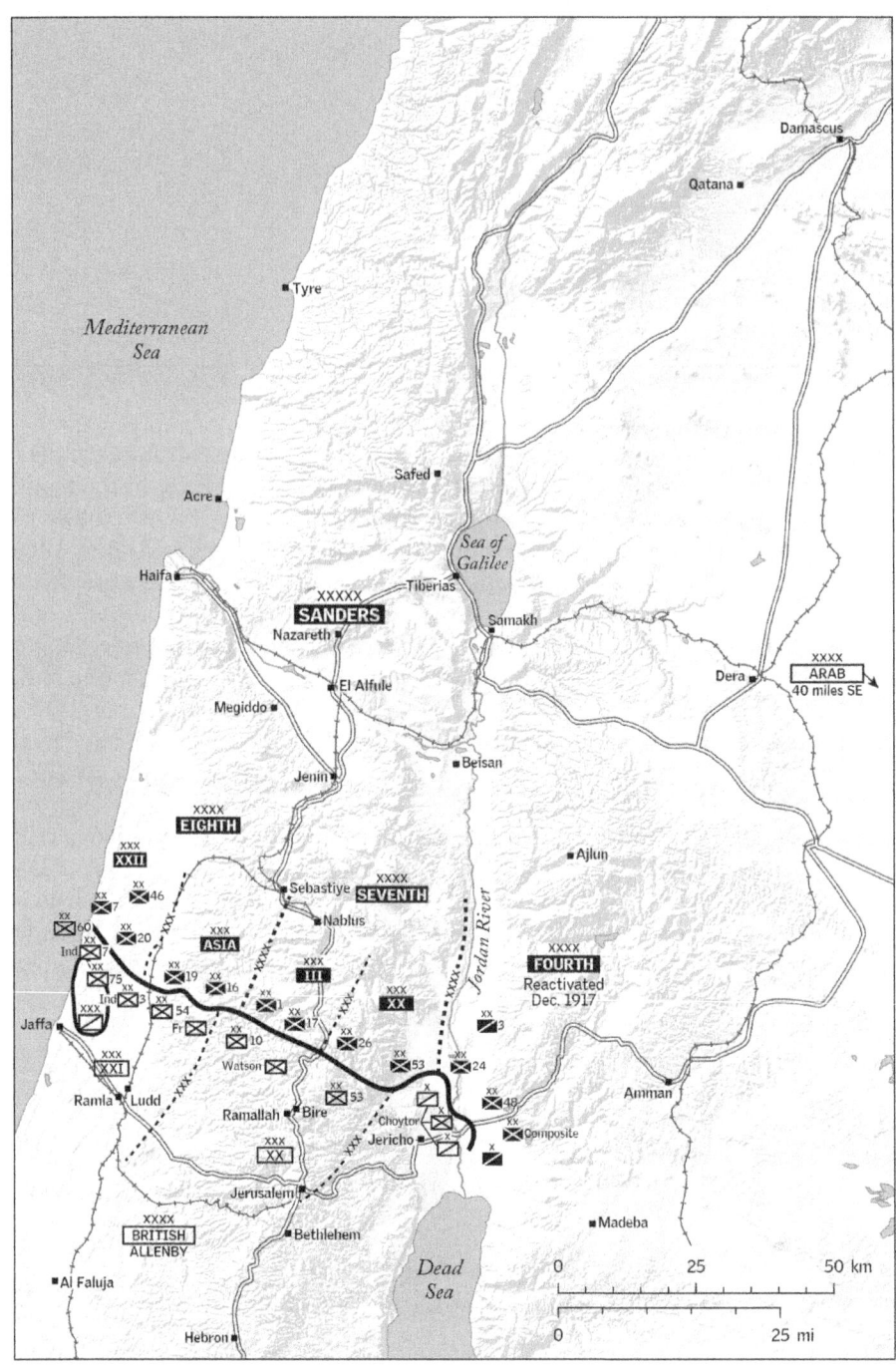

Situation 18 September 1918.

up to the Battle of Megiddo.³ This logistical net was merely an extension of the fine work done by Murray and was the key reason for the success of British operation from September 1918 until the close of the war. This, combined with the steady and orderly system for reorganization of the Egyptian Expeditionary Force, put the British in a strong position for a continuance of offensive operations in Palestine.

The Ottoman situation, by contrast, in the months leading up to the Battle of Megiddo was dire especially with regard to logistics supplying the Yildirim Army Group against British attacks. Overseeing Ottoman fortunes beginning on 27 February 1918 was Lieutenant General Otto Liman von Sanders who had gained fame for the successful Turkish defense in the 1915 Dardanelles and Gallipoli campaigns. Sanders' career, in terms of his involvement with the Ottoman Empire, started in December 1913 when he was head of the German military mission to the Turks. Upon his appointment to command Yildirim, Sanders worked tirelessly to prepare his forces for a future British offensive. This effort was handicapped from the start as the Ottomans diverted resources away from the defense of Palestine and Syria in favor of taking territory in the Caucasus to take advantage of the declining military fortunes of Russia. This situation led to a stark assessment of Turkish fortunes by General Mustapha Kemal who was appointed on 7 August 1918 to Seventh Army attached to Yildirim. Upon inspection of the sector held by his army he concluded that any future battle against the British would be lost in advance.⁴ This assessment had much to do with the troop strength of Yildirim versus that of the British. In 1918 Sanders commanded twelve under-strength infantry divisions and one cavalry division as part of the Yildirim Army Group tasked with defending a front almost 56 miles long. According to Ottoman Army doctrine, each infantry division would normally be assigned a front of three miles. As a result, Sanders should have had eighteen divisions at his disposal. Taking into account army doctrine on necessary reserves, Sanders had only ten percent of the force required to defend his front.⁵ In addition to the manpower problems, many of the troops under Sanders' command had been in the line for six months without relief.

This latter situation exacerbated the manpower problems of the Ottomans as the Yildirim group endured desertions from both troops in the line and the few reinforcements that arrived in the theater. In terms of the former, the situation proved so dire that the Ottomans began to conduct patrols behind their lines with trucks that mounted machine guns in order to deter desertion.⁶ Additional measures to guard against desertion included Turkish troops being regularly moved to different places in

---

3   Falls, *History of the Great War, based on Official Documents, Military Operations Egypt and Palestine, 1914-1918*. Volume II. *From June 1917 to the End of the War*, 440.
4   Lord Kinross, *Ataturk: A Biography of Mustapha Kemal, Father of Modern Turkey* (New York: William Morrow and Company, 1965), 137.
5   Edward Erickson, *Ottoman Army Effectiveness in World War I: A Comparative Study* (New York: Routledge, 2007), 142.
6   Falls, 445.

their defensive line. Ottoman officers hoped that this step would make sure that soldiers could not study the terrain well enough to plan a good means of deserting their posts.[7] The same problems held true for reinforcements. Large scale desertions meant that the additional troops being earmarked for the defense of Palestine and Syria were largely depleted in fighting strength before ever taking up position at the front.[8] As a result of desertion, the Ottoman Army in Palestine during 1918 grew progressively weaker. For example, due in part to desertions by summer of that year the nine infantry battalions that comprised the Ottoman 16th Infantry Division ranged in strength from 100 to 250 men. These numbers were roughly equivalent to a British infantry company.[9] Such understrength was a key reason for the outcome of the Battle of Megiddo.

Another problem exacerbating the poor fighting strength of the Yildirim Army Group in Palestine was disease. Throughout the war, the number of soldiers dying from infectious disease proved a crippling situation. According to Edward Erickson, of the 771,844 dead or missing Ottoman soldiers at the end of the war, 243,598 were combat deaths, 61,487 were missing in action, and a colossal 466,759 died from disease.[10] The Ottoman defenses north of Jerusalem were especially prone to typhus and malaria in an atmosphere of incredibly poor sanitary conditions. By the time of Megiddo, General Mustapha Kemal, in command of Seventh Army, commented on of his troops as opposed to those of the British that "We are a thread of cotton before them."[11]

In addition to severe manpower problems throughout 1918 was another factor, that of transport, which greatly impeded Ottoman efforts to defend both Palestine and Syria. Despite Ottoman efforts to improve their poor railway net to the region, logistical support remained inadequate. It was only on 9 October 1918 that the first broad gauge railroad track was made operational opposed to the limited narrow gauge track that ran through the Tarsus tunnel, being a major thoroughfare from Istanbul to points in Palestine and Syria, made operational.[12] The rest of the railway net remained the same broken system that contained a myriad of gauges of track that necessitated the constant offloading and on loading of supplies to different trains. Added to the poor state of the railway was the terrible status of the Turkish Camel Transport Corps. Over the course of the war the Turks lost 40,000 animals in Palestine and Syria due to bad conditions in their stables, starvation, and disease.[13]

---

7   Great Britain, National Archives, GHQ Intelligence Summary, 5 September 1918, WO 157/731.
8   Kinross, 138.
9   Edward Erickson, *Ottoman Army Effectiveness in World War I*, 132.
10 Edward Erickson, *Ordered to Die: A History of the Ottoman Army in the First World War* (London: Greenwood Press, 2001), 211. See also Hikmet Özdemir, *The Ottoman Army, 1914-1918: Disease and Death on the Battlefield* (Salt Lake City, UT: University of Utah Press, 2008), 127-128.
11 Kinross, 138.
12 H. Pirie Gordon, *A Brief Record of the Advance of the Egyptian Expeditionary Force* (London, HMSO: 1919), 230.
13 Badcock, 56.

As the British Egyptian Expeditionary Force grew in strength in relation to the growing weakness of the Ottomans, General Allenby began in July 1918 to contemplate further offensive operations in a push past the Gaza-Beersheba line that included that which became the Battle of Megiddo. His plans centered on an assault in Palestine to take place sometime in September. Not only was this consideration a product of the requirements to reorganize effectively the Egyptian Expeditionary Force, but it was also a calculation that took into account the weather for an offensive. Allenby knew that rains came to his theater beginning in early November while the weather just before was optimal for operations. As an illustration, the meteorological reports in the days just before the Battle of Megiddo predicted light wind with a temperature between 77 and 90 degrees Fahrenheit, no rain, and humidity ranging from 69 to 86 percent.[14] Allenby's attention to the weather is no great surprise. During his deployment with the Egyptian Expeditionary Force, Allenby carried with him only two books: the Bible and George Smith's *The Historical Geography of the Holy Land* that detailed all aspects of Palestine including weather. The first operation that Allenby proposed was one that was limited in scope: an offensive to establish a line between Nablus in eastern Palestine and Tulkarem in the west. In his dispatch to Chief of the Imperial General Staff Wilson on 24 July 1918 Allenby asserted the importance of this drive lay in Nablus and Tulkarem being the headquarters of the Turkish Seventh and Eighth Armies. These towns also lay astride the Ottoman logistical net, which meant that denying supplies to the enemy would weaken their overall defense of the theater. Finally, Allenby asserted that a successful drive would encourage his new Indian troops and bolster Britain's Arab allies.[15] Wilson proved generally supportive of Allenby's plan.

Consequently, Allenby unveiled on 1 August 1918 secret orders to his corps commanders for an operation to seize the Nablus-Tulkarem line. While a limited plan, it did hold similarities to the scheme that ultimately produced the Battle of Megiddo.[16] In the first stage of the operation the XXI Corps of the Egyptian Expeditionary Force, with five divisions under Lieutenant General Bulfin, was to break through the Turkish flank in the Plain of Sharon on the coastline of the Mediterranean Sea. Once Turkish lines were breached, Lieutenant General Chauvel's Desert Mounted Corps with three cavalry divisions would exploit the breach and advance northward to the region of the Nahr Iskanderune before swinging eastward for a drive to Sebustiye with the support of one division of the XXI Corps. The capture of Sebustiye would sever the railway supply line to Nablus in preparation for a drive on that town. This plan rested on the idea of massing troops and cavalry near the sea since Allenby's

---

14 Great Britain, National Archives, GHQ Intelligence Summary, "Meteorological Report for the week ending on 14 September 1918," 14 September 1918, WO157/731.
15 Allenby to Wilson, 24 July 1918, in Matthew Hughes, *Allenby in Palestine: The Middle East Correspondence of Field Marshal Viscount Allenby, June 1917-October 1919* (Stroud: Sutton Publishing, 2004), 168-169.
16 See Falls, 448-449.

prior experience with operations in the Jordan Valley convinced him of that necessity. Whilst the Plain of Sharon was flat, the geography of the Jordan Valley was horrendous. Allenby's plan relied on the need for speed in order to accomplish his objectives in the face of the Turkish defenders. From prior experience, the rate of advance in the Jordan Valley was no more than five miles a day.[17]

This plan was only an embryonic one. Then on 22 August 1918 Allenby greatly extended the goal of the campaign. His revised plan envisioned not merely extending British defensive lines north, but an operation that would completely destroy Ottoman defenses in Palestine.[18] Like the first plan, it centered on a massed infantry attack by the XXI Corps near the coastline. It also included an advance of the Desert Mounted Corps, located to the rear of the XXI Corps, northward on the Plain of Sharon. In this scheme, the XXI Corps, with one cavalry brigade attached, would assume one central task previously allotted to the Desert Mounted Corps: the capture of Sebustiye and an advance on Nablus. The reason was that Allenby gave the Desert Mounted Corps a far more distant northern objective. Chauvel's command would ride along the coastline, disregarding any enemy force that did not lie directly in its path, until reaching the Nahr el Mefjir and then turn northeast through two passes into the Plain of Esdraelon in the rear of Turkish defenses. From there, the Desert Mounted Corps would occupy Afule, some 45 miles north of the British line, and Beisan, being 60 miles distant, as well as send a detachment to Nazareth, the headquarters of General Liman von Sanders of Yildirim, in an attempt to capture him. While this unfolded, the XX Corps farther to the east on the British line would march on Nablus. On the far right flank a small force was to defend the Jordan Valley while the Arab allies of the British, under the command of Emir Feisal, would cut Turkish communications north and west of the central Turkish railway hub of Deraa. In essence, Allenby's plan was one that relied very heavily on speed through massed cavalry to cut off the logistical net of the Turkish army groups defending Palestine, encircle them, and destroy them as they attempted to retreat north. The destruction of the Turkish forces was exactly what Allenby desired as he made this goal known to his commanders over the next seven weeks. An example was his statement to them that: "There are no objectives, but I want the whole of the Turkish army, and I am going to have it."[19] The plan relied on an elastic system of advance without restraining timetables as the advance of each force was dependent on the varying degrees of success of the others.

The one great risk centered on the Egyptian Expeditionary Force's logistical net to supply the offensive. The answer to the problem lay in meticulous planning to make sure that the Egyptian Expeditionary Force had the supplies necessary at the beginning of the offensive. Of particular concern was supply for the Desert Mounted Corps, which

---

17 Gordon, 38.
18 Archibald Wavell, *The Palestine Campaigns* (London: Constable, 1928), 198-200.
19 Raymond Savage, *Allenby of Armageddon: The Career and Campaigns of Field Marshal Viscount Allenby* (Indianapolis: Bobbs-Merrill, 1926), 291.

was the crux of the operation. Its advance would carry far beyond the logistical net of the Egyptian Expeditionary Force. As a result, the British paid particular attention to supplies that could be carried by the cavalry themselves. This plan centered on the normal day's ration of the force, an iron ration of canned meat and biscuits, and two days of emergency rations carried on the horses as well as in wagons.[20] Water for the horses and soldiers alike was another matter. In the weeks leading up to the assault, British intelligence did its best to identify all water wells in enemy territory for use not only of the Desert Mounted Corps, but also the infantry.[21]

Whilst the issue of the proper supply for British forces in the enemy rear was a concern, one logistical problem that did not exist was that of poor supply at the front during the beginning of the operation. Over the months following the capture of Jerusalem, Allenby continued to direct efforts to extend and improve on the fine logistical system, created by his predecessor, that extended from Egypt. The only existing metaled road in Palestine south of the Jaffa-Jerusalem line before the summer of 1918 was the one at Beersheba and even this one stretched for several miles where there was nothing but the road bed. Motorized transport was a problem given this situation. As a result, Allenby directed the collection of stone from quarries for the construction of new roads and strengthened culverts for bridges over the many wadis of the region to support motorized transport. These efforts proved particularly valuable and by the end of the war the Egyptian Expeditionary Force operated 5,905 mechanized vehicles.[22] Allenby oversaw many of these preparations personally. In the months leading up to the Battle of Megiddo, Allenby "covered many hundreds of miles in his car…and especially so in the months of June, July, and August."[23] Also, the British continued to improve their railroad net for the transport of supplies to the front. By the first half of September the railroad carried forward to Ludd while the pre-existing Turkish narrow gauge line that extended from Ludd to Jerusalem was rebuilt for British broad gauge railroad cars.[24] Finally, the British extended the water pipeline north while British troops on the front dug wells in search of water wherever there was promise. In the beach sector of the line held by the XXI Corps, the 60th Division dug 45 wells that each provided 3,000 gallons of water a day.[25] Allenby hoped that these efforts would at least ensure that his forces had the supplies they needed for the initial assault. Allenby also envisioned using the Ottoman's logistical net for his troops. Allenby in the days before the Battle of Megiddo issued directives to all his commanders to keep

20   Cyril Falls, *Armageddon 1918* (London: Weidenfeld and Nicolson, 1964), 53.
21   Great Britain, National Archives, GHQ Intelligence Summary, 11 September 1918, WO 157/731, 2-3.
22   Badcock, 185-186. See also Gordon, 108.
23   Gordon, 319.
24   R.M.P. Preston, *The Desert Mounted Corps: An Account of the Cavalry Operations in Palestine and Syria, 1917-1918* (New York: Houghton Mifflin, 1923), 190-191.
25   Vivian Gilbert, *The Romance of the Last Crusade: With Allenby to Jerusalem* (New York: D. Appleton, 1923), 223.

intact as much as possible the road systems of the Ottomans during the advance of the Egyptian Expeditionary Force. This extended to making sure that as many telegraph lines were preserved as possible for British communication in the field.[26]

Supplementing the efforts to use the Turkish supply net for their own gain was the exhaustive intelligence efforts to map out these assets through both aerial reconnaissance and interrogation of Turkish prisoners of war. Not only did this aid British logistical efforts in the field during the Battle of Megiddo, but it also greatly facilitated the successful operation of British troops against the Turks as a whole. Air power proved crucial as the Royal Air Force steadily gained dominance of the skies over Turkish positions in the months leading up to the Battle of Megiddo. In June 1918, 100 Turkish and German aircraft crossed over Allenby's lines, but by the last week of August that number had been reduced to only 18 aircraft.[27] With mastery of the skies, the Royal Flying Corps of the Palestinian Brigade was assigned the task of collecting all data possible on Turkish installations as well as the topography that lay north of the British line. The pictures taken by the reconnaissance planes were of particularly high quality as the aircraft beginning in December 1917 had wide angle cameras on new mounts that greatly reduced vibration from the aircraft that could affect the quality of the picture. The pilots of the brigade produced priceless intelligence for the Battle of Megiddo. In 1918, they surveyed almost 1,236 square miles beyond the British front. Over the first ten months of 1918, 16,000 negatives produced over a quarter of a million photographs for use in the field. This intelligence data led to the publication of the "Handbook on Northern Palestine and Southern Syria" and the "Topography of Central Syria" in April 1918. By the beginning September 1918, the British possessed a comprehensive map of the strategic zone north of their position to a depth of 31 miles.[28] This included the key regions around Afule and Beisan on which hinged British fortunes in the Battle of Megiddo. In addition to aerial intelligence was that gleaned from Turkish defectors and prisoners of war. Not only were these questioned concerning Turkish troop strength, but interrogators required them to supply any information they knew concerning water supplies behind Turkish lines.[29] By the opening of the Battle of Megiddo, Allenby knew a great deal about both the enemy and the topography that lay before him. His intelligence only got two things wrong. One was an overestimation of the size of Turkish forces while another was a great underestimation of the number of machine guns at the disposal of the Turks. Neither of these proved significant enough to alter the outcome of the battle.

Along with good preparation was the need for secrecy and deception in order for the operation to be a British success. While the British Expeditionary Force enjoyed a great preponderance in troops and supplies over the Ottomans, if the Turks could

---

26 Great Britain, National Archives, Diaries of the GHQ Egyptian Expeditionary Force, 7 September 1918, WO 95/4371.
27 Preston, 198.
28 Yigal Sheffy, *British Military Intelligence in the Palestinian Campaign, 1914-1918* (London: Frank Cass, 1998), 305, 315.
29 Sheffy, 316.

find out the point of the attack they could mass their troops to meet it. Any Turkish knowledge in this regard would at least slow the rate of the operation to the point where the Desert Mounted Corps might not be able to reach the Plain of Esdraelon in time to envelop the retreating Turks. An illustration of the need for deception is the secrecy surrounding the operation. While the corps commanders knew all the details of the offensive, Allenby ordered that they share the complete details of the plan with only those who absolutely needed to know:

> The Commander-in Chief wished to remind you that, when it becomes necessary to explain to Commanding Officers the plans for the future operations, the information given to them should be limited strictly to what is essential of them to know, in order to play their part. At the same time they should be warned that all officers and the rank and file should be kept in ignorance until the last moment and should then be told only so much as will enable them to carry out their immediate task.[30]

Only after 9 September did junior officers find out the complete details of their operations. This insured that no intelligence leaked to the enemy.

In addition to general secrecy, deception was used to mask the movement of cavalry from sectors of the British front to the coastline. A key to this deception was the efforts made to make the Ottomans think that the impending British assault would be directed in the Jordan Valley rather than the coastline. This effort began on 16 August when the headquarters of the Desert Mounted Corps was closed at Tala ted Damm on the Jerusalem to Jericho road and re-opened at Jerishe. In terms of the cavalry, Allenby issued orders to General Chaytor's force on the far right flank of the British defenses in the Jordan Valley to make preparations with his troops as though an attack in the area was imminent. Meanwhile, Chauvel's cavalry made demonstrations in the region of the Jordan Valley while simultaneously the bulk of his forces moved west.[31] The Palestinian Brigade of the Royal Air Force made this operation possible. During the concentration of force, only four Turkish airplanes managed to cross over British lines. This situation was in part the result of the fact that by 19 September the Turks had only five aircraft capable of aerial reconnaissance. The glaring problem was one voiced on 3 September by Colonel Gustav von Oppen of the German Asia Korps, a unit that was part of the Ottoman defenses, where he requested greater aerial reconnaissance because German planes were being shot down over his lines which greatly affected the morale of his troops.[32]

---

30 Great Britain, National Archives, Diaries of the GHQ Egyptian Expeditionary Force, 9 September 1918, WO 95/4371.
31 See Australian War Memorial, Diaries of the 2nd Australian Light Horse, 14 September 1918, AWM4 10/2/45, and Great Britain, National Archives, Diaries of the GHQ Egyptian Expeditionary Force, 5 September 1918, WO 95/4371.
32 Liman von Sanders, *Five Years in Turkey* (Annapolis: Naval Institute Press, 1927),, 273.

Assets moved steadily west, and while under this air cover Chaytor pursued elaborate operations to convince the Ottomans that the point of attack was indeed in the Jordan Valley rather than the coast. Among these efforts was the construction of 15,000 dummy horses covered by canvas as well as riders to make it appear as though the entire Desert Mounted Corps was on the right flank of the British line. In addition, the camps for the cavalry were kept standing after the departure of the corps with their campfires burning at night. Finally, the British used mules pulling sleighs to raise dust to simulate a massive movement of cavalry in the Jordan Valley. Small detachments of British troops supplemented the work of these mules.[33] The Turks consequently believed that the British were massing their forces in a region where there were progressively fewer and fewer forces. Strengthening the ruse was the British use of wireless transmissions, broadcast in the open, which suggested a relocation of the General Headquarters of the Egyptian Expeditionary Force. Finally, Captain T.E. Lawrence, the liaison between the British and their Arab allies, sent agents to Amman in the Jordan Valley to buy all available horse feed in the region while stating to the local people that it was for the maintenance of British cavalry in the area.[34]

As the deception unfolded, the cavalry moved to the coastline in five consecutive night marches that averaged 14 miles a march. While this greatly tired the troops, the concentration proved a success as the orange groves around Ramleh, Jaffa, and Ludd began to teem with horses and their riders: 'Every night the plain was alive with columns of all arms moving westward.'[35] In addition to the cavalry, infantry of the 60th Division also moved to the same orange groves. Not only did these groves provide cover for the British in order to conceal their movements, but these regions also contained irrigation systems that could water horses and troops alike.

The Ottomans remained almost entirely ignorant of these troop movements until the onset of the Battle of Megiddo. As late as 29 August the Turks believed that a British offensive was imminent, but that it would unfold in the Jordan Valley with the objective being the railway depot at Deraa.[36] Only in two instances did the Ottomans gain intelligence that the British were massing for an attack in an area other than the Jordan Valley. One of these was a 15 September account of one of the few German airmen that flew over British lines. It reported that there was a regrouping of British cavalry to the left flank of their line. Even so, the report suggested that this was not a mass movement.[37] The other report resulted from the 17 September desertion of Sepoy

---

33 Falls, *History of the Great War*, 462.
34 H.S. Gullet, *The Official History of Australia in the War of 1914-1918*, Vol. 7, *Sinai and Palestine: The Australian Imperial Force in Sinai and Palestine, 1914-1918* (Sydney: Angus and Robertson, 1923), 687.
35 T. Gibbons, *With the 1/5th Essex in the East* (Colchester, UK: Benham, 1921), 135.
36 Great Britain, National Archives, "Translation of a Document Captured by Desert Mounted Corps During Operations 19th to 21st September, 1918," WO 157/735.
37 Gullet, 687.

Ujagar Singh of the Sikh Pioneers who revealed the date, hour, and direction of the attack. The Turks, however, discounted this intelligence as a ruse.[38] Even so, General Mustapha Kemal of the Ottoman Seventh Army gave it enough credence to call a meeting of his staff in which he ordered them to be ready for an attack in the early morning of 19 September. Kemal sent a copy of this order to Liman von Sanders, who while not fully believing that an attack would occur on that day, did communicate that at least it never hurt to be prepared.[39] Such preparation was certainly wise as Sanders knew that an attack was imminent, but not the direction.

This situation was a dire one for the Ottomans and a tribute to the British efforts at deception. As a result of not knowing the direction of the impending attack, Ottoman lines had to stay un-concentrated throughout their defensive line. Sanders saw this as a potential problem given the lack of reserve forces available to the Yildirim Army Group. In September, the only divisions available for reserve service were the 2nd Caucasian Cavalry Division in the area of the Eighth Army that occupied the coastal sector and the 3rd Cavalry Division in the area of the Fourth Army in Jordan.[40] Additionally, there were no secondary lines of defense in order to stage a fighting withdrawal if necessary. In light of thin Ottoman lines and reserves, in the weeks prior to receiving the intelligence that suggested a British offensive, Sanders had contemplated a strategic withdrawal north to center a new line on Lake Tiberias.[41] Sanders, however, being an individual who was a proponent of trench warfare and dedicated to holding ground at all costs, stayed wedded to the idea of a static defense of his existing lines. Reinforcing his decision was the low morale and poor supply of Yildirim forces that would greatly exacerbate any difficulties caused by a strategic withdrawal with food being a key problem. By 1 September 1918 the Ottoman Eighth Army had only 14.5 tons of flour available, which was wholly inadequate for the force.[42] This lack of food was not only the result of the poor logistical net of the Ottoman Army but was also due to two other factors. One was the British naval blockade of the Ottoman Empire that greatly increased the price of food. Another was an event that occurred at least a year before the Battle of Megiddo. On 6 September 1917, an explosion at Haidar Pasha Station near Istanbul had destroyed nearly all of the stores and munitions earmarked for the Yildirim Army Group.[43] In terms of combat efficiency,

---

38   Great Britain, British Library, Oriental and India Office Collections, "Nominal Rolls of Indian Prisoners of War, Suspected of Having Deserted to the Enemy or of Having Given Information to or Otherwise Assisted the Enemy After Capture: Egyptian Expeditionary Force," L/MIL/17/5/2403, 3.
39   Kinross, 139.
40   Erickson, *Ordered to Die*, 196.
41   See Sanders, 273-274 and Erickson, *Ottoman Army Effectiveness*, 142-143.
42   Erickson, *Ottoman Army Effectiveness*, 133.
43   See Archibald C Bell, *A History of the Blockade of Germany and of the Countries Associated with Her in the Great War: Austria-Hungary, Bulgaria, Turkey, 1914-1918* (London: Her Majesty's Stationary Office, 1961), 579-580 for a discussion of the blockade. See Falls, *Armageddon 1918*, 42 for coverage of the explosion at Haidar Pasha.

the problem with disease was exacerbated by the lack of food. Indeed, the lack of food contributed to the rate of disease as malnourished soldiers became increasingly vulnerable to illness.

As a result of their host of problems which the British did not experience, the Yildirim Army Group was wholly unprepared for the Battle of Megiddo. In August 1918 the Yildirim Army Group had 40,598 infantry, 370 artillery pieces, 273 light machine guns, and 696 heavy machine guns.[44] These forces occupied an area 45 miles in length from the coast to the Jordan Valley. From west to east, the Eighth Army under the command of General Djevad Pasha was comprised of the 46th Division along with the XXII Corps that was comprised of the 7th and 20th Divisions. They held a front that ran from the sea to about twenty miles inland. This 8,000-man force, with its headquarters at Tul Karm, bore the brunt of the British initial thrust in the Battle of Megiddo. The German Asia Korps made up of the 16th and 19th divisions of Colonel von Oppen lay just east of the Eighth Army while farther east lay the Seventh Army of General Mustapha Kemal. This force, headquartered at Nablus, had two corps: The III Corps with the 1st and 11th divisions and the XX Corps comprising the 24th, 26th, and 53rd divisions. Beyond the Jordan Valley was the last of the Turkish defenses, being that of the Fourth Army under the command of General Mohammad Jemal Pasha that comprised the 3rd Cavalry Division, the II Corps containing the Hauran Detachment, the Amman Detachment, and the Ma'an Detachment, and the VIII Corps composed of the 48th Division and Caucasus Cavalry Brigade. In command of all Yildirim forces was General Liman von Sanders with his General Headquarters based at Nazareth. The site Sanders chosen for his base proved one of the final problems for the Ottomans in the Battle of Megiddo. Not only was Nazareth too far away from the front, but the nearest railroad station of El Afule was a little over six miles away. These two facts combined meant that "conditions for transmitting orders and for receiving reports, and the personal supervision of the heads of the staff sections, were very difficult and retarding."[45] Given the speed in which the Battle of Megiddo unfolded, Sanders at his central command was largely not an effective force for command and control.

The Yildirim Army Group faced a well-supplied and trained Egyptian Expeditionary Force that numbered 12,000 cavalry, 57,000 infantry, and 540 artillery pieces.[46] Bearing the brunt of the assault was the Desert Mounted Corps and the XXI Corps in the coastal sectors. The Desert Mounted Corps, under the command of Lieutenant General Sir H.G. Chauvel, comprised the 4th and 5th Cavalry Divisions as well as the Australian Mounted Division. The XXI Corps commanded by Lieutenant General Sir E.S. Bulfin contained the 3rd Indian Lahore Division, the 7th Indian Meerut

---

44   Erickson, *Ordered to Die*, 196. See also Cyril Falls, *History of the Great War*, 452.
45   Werner Steuber, *Jildirim: Deutsche Streiter auf helligem Boden* (Oldenburg, Stalling, 1924), 11.
46   Cyril Falls, *History of the Great War*, 452.

Division, the 54th East Anglian Division and the 60th and 75th divisions. Under Bulfin's command was also the Detachment Francais de Palestine et Syrie, being a small French force. Further east in the center of the British line was the XX Corps of Lieutenant General Sir P.W. Chetwode that comprised the 10th and 53rd divisions. The final portion of the British line, as well as the smallest, lay in the region of the Jordan Valley under the command of Major General Sir E.W.C. Chaytor. His command comprised the Australian and New Zealand Mounted Division as well as battalion and brigade strength infantry formations. All these forces collectively were poised for an offensive beginning on 19 September.

4

Battle

The Battle of Megiddo hinged on XXI Corps' component infantry divisions punching a hole through Ottoman defenses and then a sweeping cavalry charge by the Desert Mounted Corps through the created gap. The offensive commenced with aerial operations and an artillery bombardment to disrupt Turkish communications and degrade the Ottoman defenses. Allenby's plan called for a heavy use of British air superiority against the Turks. The first blow of the operation came from the 1st Squadron Australian Flying Corps of the Palestinian Brigade Royal Air Force. At 1:00 AM on 19 September, this unit dropped 16 hundredweight bombs on the railroad junction of Afule while firing 850 machine gun rounds at the Ottoman aerodrome in the region.[1] Similar attacks later in the day occurred at Tul Karm, headquarters of the Ottoman Eighth Army, Nablus, the headquarters of the Ottoman Seventh Army, and against the aerodrome at Jenin.

These attacks proved devastating in two respects. They were so effective that the Ottomans were able to get only one plane airborne on 19 September and another airborne on 20 September for the sake of reconnaissance. This situation created a severe lack of knowledge on the positions of British forces during the offensive and greatly handicapped the Ottoman defense of Palestine. In addition, the bombing of army headquarters and railroad stations such as Afule severely disrupted Ottoman communications and thus exacerbated the same problem. By 7:00 AM on 19 September communication between Yildirim's headquarters and Tul Karm ended. By between 9:00 AM and 10:00 AM the Ottoman Seventh Army headquarters at Nablus reported that British cavalry were riding through the Plain of Sharon. Indeed, it was not until 8:50 AM that Liman von Sanders heard anything about the British offensive as the phone lines from his headquarters to his corps commanders had been cut by British bombing. By the end of the first day of the Battle of Megiddo, the Royal Air Force had dropped eleven tons of bombs and fired 66,000 rounds of ammunition

---

1   Australian War Memorial, Diary of the 1st Squadron Australian Flying Corps, 19 September 1918, AWM 4 8/4/9.

Battle 67

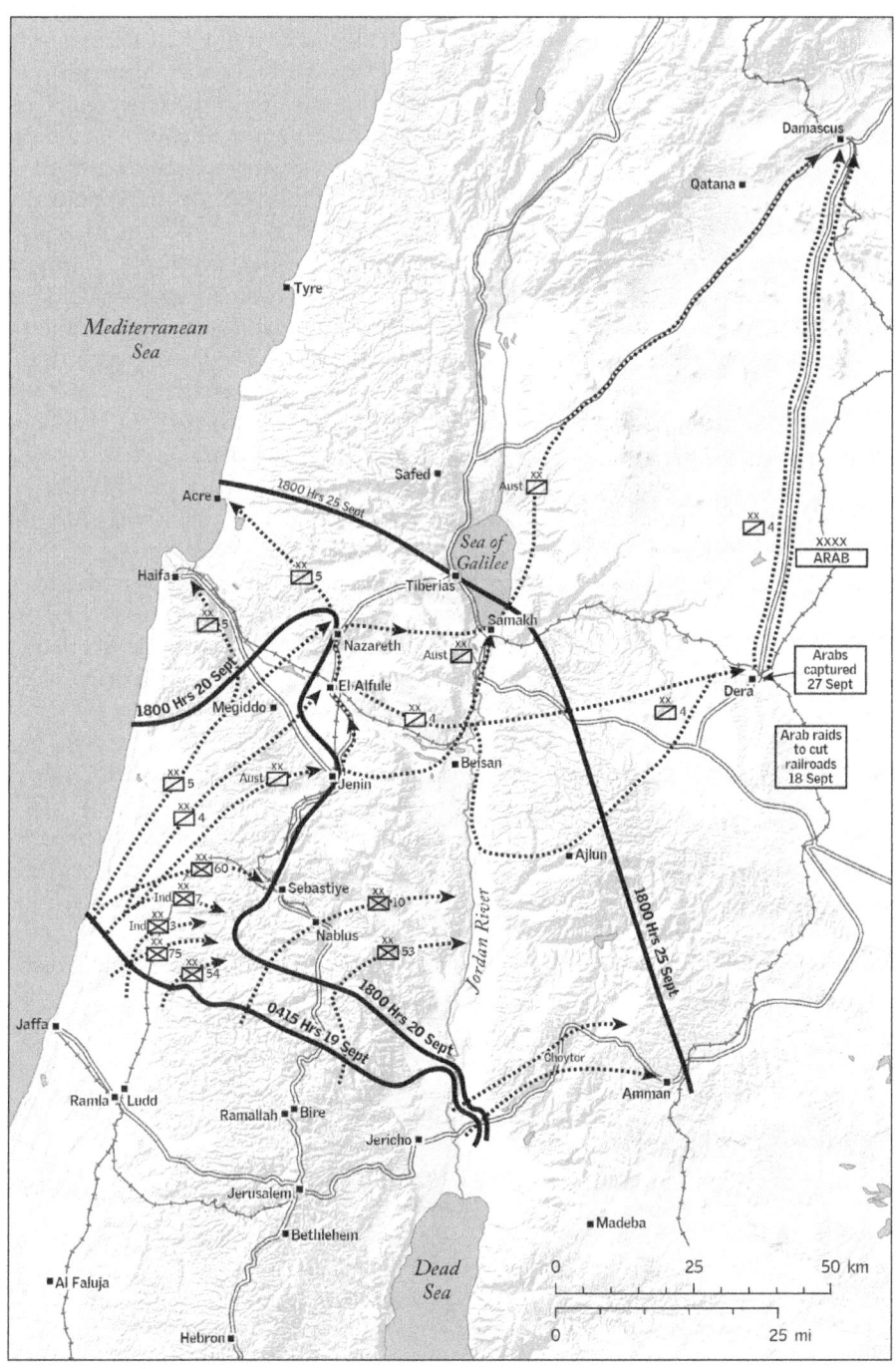

Situation 19 September–31 October 1918.

at ground positions. This situation was one which the Turks could do little to counter. Not only did they not have planes in the air, but the entire Turkish army manning the front had only two anti-aircraft guns at their disposal.[2] Even these two guns were not effective against British aircraft. The reason was the poor quality of the ammunition used for the guns. British intelligence translated a captured document from the Ottoman Eighth Army dated 27 May 1918 that stated fully 60% of the rounds fired failed to explode.[3]

As the Palestinian Brigade Royal Air Force began their efforts against the Ottomans so too did the artillery of the Egyptian Expeditionary Force. Allenby assigned the bulk of his artillery to Bulfin's XXI Corps in order to achieve the penetration of Ottoman defenses necessary for the charge of the Desert Mounted Corps. Bulfin had at his disposal 258 guns and 126 howitzers. About three quarters of these were concentrated on a seven-mile front between Jaffa on the coast and the Tul Karm road to the east.[4] These guns clearly outmatched those of the Turks in terms of what the latter could bring to bear in counter battery fire. On the eve of the offensive, the Ottomans fielded 120 artillery pieces in the region of the British offensive as Allenby's measures of deception resulted in Turkish artillery still being spread throughout their defensive lines.[5] The disparity between British and Ottoman guns was even greater. Supplementing British artillery was the Royal Navy with two destroyers, the *Druid* and the *Forester*. Allenby tasked the captains of these vessels to provide fire support for the 60th Division, since they were the closest to the sea as part of the drive of XXI Corps. Once the breakthrough was achieved, these destroyers had orders to proceed north in support of the Desert Mounted Corps with particular attention being paid to the port of Haifa.[6] Both these destroyers and the land-based artillery had orders to begin bombardment at 4:30 a.m. on 19 September 1918.

The conditions for the artillery barrage proved perfect as the artillery opened up on Turkish positions on a bright, moonlit night firing 1,000 shells per minute. These shells were high explosive rather than gas shells even though on the eve of Megiddo the Egyptian Expeditionary Force had stockpiled 100,000 chlorine gas shells.[7] Unlike bombardments that characterized early offensives in theaters such as the Western

---

2   Lawrence James, *Imperial Warrior: The Life and Times of Field-Marshal Viscount Allenby,1861-1936* (London: Weidenfeld and Nicolson, 1993), 166.
3   Great Britain, National Archives, GHQ Intelligence Summary, 25 September 1918, WO 157/731.
4   Cyril Falls, *History of the Great War, based on Official Documents, Military Operations Egypt and Palestine, 1914-1918*. Volume II. *From June 1917 to the End of the War* (London: HMSO, 1930), 456.
5   Edward Erickson, *Ordered to Die: A History of the Ottoman Army in the First World War* (London: Greenwood Press, 2001), 198.
6   Great Britain, National Archives, Diaries of the GHQ Egyptian Expeditionary Force, "Instructions for HMS Forrester and Druid", 15 September 1918, WO 95/4371.
7   Yigal Sheffy, "Chemical Warfare and the Palestine Campaign, 1916-1918", *The Journal of Military History*, July 2009, Volume 73, Number 3, pp. 841.

Front, this was not a preliminary bombardment prior to the infantry assault. Instead, it served as the signal for Bulfin's XXI Corps to advance on Turkish positions. The British infantry assault hinged on the XXI Corps' 60th, 75th, 3rd Indian, and 7th Indian divisions versus initially the Ottoman 7th and 20th divisions of the Ottoman Eighth Army. In total, the 8,000 men of General Djevad Pasha's Eighth Army faced a concerted British assault of 35,000 infantry and 9,000 cavalry.[8] The orders for Bulfin's forces was to advance eight miles to the foothills southeast of Jijulieh. After this advance opened a gap in Turkish defenses, the infantry of XXI Corps was to swing right and advance northeast to strike against an area northwest of Nablus. General Archibald Wavell likened this movement to opening a door where the handle was at the coast and the hinges were in the foothills east in order to allow the cavalry through.[9] Not only would this pave the way for the cavalry, but Allenby also intended the infantry offensive to push the Ottoman Eighth Army up the Nablus-Jenin road in retreat where they would be enveloped by the Desert Mounted Corps as they passed north through the Plain of Esdraelon, thus encircling them. The drive would also threaten the Ottoman Seventh Army's communications through the advance to Nablus. Before dawn's light, Turkish counter battery fire had ceased as British infantry marched through the one mile of No Man's Land that separated the opposing lines and swarmed into Turkish trenches to accomplish their task.

On the extreme west of the British drive lay the 60th Division commanded by Major General J.S.M. Shea that advanced in two columns on Turkish defenses. At 4:40 AM one company of the Kumaon Rifles overran the Turkish line west of Birket Atife in only two minutes, taking 110 prisoners and eight machine guns.[10] Passing to their east was the 180th Brigade of which the Kumaon Rifles were a part. They advanced at the rate of 75 yards per minute behind the British artillery barrage. The 60th Division accomplished all of its initial objectives rather quickly. The efforts of the division allowed the 5th Cavalry Division of the Desert Mounted Corps to ride into the Plain of Sharon at 7:30 AM, only three hours into the operation.[11] At this point units of the 60th Division began a right wheel turn east towards Tul Karm, which they captured at 5:00 p.m., in an atmosphere where the division had caused great damage to the Ottoman Eighth Army. While Ottoman casualties were at the time unknown, on the first day of operations the 60th Division took 1,280 Ottoman prisoners of war, 19 artillery pieces, and 29 machine guns.[12] These numbers represented a significant portion of the operational strength of the Ottoman Eighth Army.

---

8   Edward Erickson, *Ottoman Army Effectiveness in World War I: A Comparative Study* (New York: Routledge, 2007), 146.
9   Archibald Wavell, *The Palestine Campaigns* (London: Constable, 1941), 273.
10 Falls, *History of the Great War*, 485.
11 P.H. Dalbiac, *History of the 60th Division* (London: George Allen and Unwin, 1927), 226.
12 Great Britain, National Archives, Diaries of the General Staff 60th Division, WO 95/4660.

Immediately to the east of the 60th Division lay the 7th Meerut Division under the command of Major General Sir V.B. Fane. His orders for the first day of operations entailed the capture of the enemy's front-line positions in a sector that lay between a wadi west of Tabor and the Wadi Hurab el Miske. He was then to break through the defenses near Et Tire that lay to the immediate left of the adjacent 75th Division. The units of the 7th Division ultimately enjoyed similar success to those of the 60th Division, although the advance proved more difficult. While the assault caught the Turks by surprise, since the division did not take their starting positions 500 yards from the enemy until just before the artillery barrage, the advance was hindered by Turkish Very Lights that sparked a brush fire and broke up the formation of the advance for the first 300 yards. Additionally, the smoke of the fire and the dust raised by the advance itself contributed to what was a halting advance.[13] The geography of the region also proved a challenge because of the low, open flats that led up to Turkish defenses that sat on the sand ridges. Even so, the division took its first objectives at 4:50 AM as the 92nd Punjabi Regiment took Turkish positions.[14] By the end of the first day of operations, owing to the difficulties of the advance, the division had accomplished their objective despite the men being exhausted and in need of water. The exhaustion felt by the troops was of such a magnitude that they could not pursue enemy soldiers as they conducted a wholesale retreat: "a party of Germans were seen moving off and escaped scot free, though Lewis guns were turned on them."[15] Even so, the division had covered 16 miles in day one and accomplished its objectives.

The 75th Division commanded by Major General P.C. Palin to the east of the 7th Meerut had as its primary target Et Tire. This assault proved more difficult than that of the 60th and 7th divisions as the area had a great deal of cactus hedges that slowed the British advance. The greatest resistance lay at a wadi southwest of Miske where three batteries of Turkish artillery kept up very intense fire against the 1/152 Indian Infantry Regiment to a range of 60 yards. At that range, the Indians conducted a successful bayonet charge that capture three 150mm howitzers, seven 77mm guns, and all of the detachments assigned to them.[16] By the end of the day, the soldiers of the 75th Division had advanced five miles and captured Et Tire, but suffered 518 casualties. Out of this total of casualties, 352 came from the 232nd Brigade alone.

To the east of the 75th Division was the 3rd Lahore Division under Major General A.R. Hoskins whose job was to break through Turkish defenses at Sabiye before turning east to march on Jaljulye. As with the experience of the 75th Division, one of the biggest challenges besides the Turkish defenders was the geography of the area. The area of the front was rather sandy, making visibility low as the high explosive shells of Turkish artillery blew sand into the air. The halting advance of the infantry,

---

13 Great Britain, National Archives, Diary of the 1st Seaforth Highlanders Regiment, 7th Meerut Division, WO 95/4712.
14 Great Britain, National Archives, Diary of the 92nd Punjabi Regiment, WO 95/4712.
15 Great Britain, National Archives, Diaries of the 7th Meerut Division, WO 95/4712.
16 Falls, *History of the Great* War, 481.

beginning at 4:27 AM, thus occurred in a situation where the leading troops of the division could only see 15 yards ahead of them. Progress on the division's left flank was particularly slow as British troops encountered portions of Colonel von Oppen's German Asia Korps. By the end of 19 September, the division like the others had accomplished its objectives, but it had taken 20 hours of hard fighting. The condition of the soldiers at the end of the first day's fighting was much like that of the 7th Meerut Division. One soldier commented that "my platoon was composed of the stoutest hearted men imaginable and they did their damndest---but they were now almost dropping with fatigue…Once on their allotted position they just flopped and slept the moment they touched the ground."[17]

The final division involved in the British wheel to the east against Turkish defenses was the 54th East Anglian Division under the command of Major General S. W. Hare. The division had orders to advance with the French Detachment Francais de Palestine et Syrie, under the command of Colonel P. de Piepape, on the right flank. In the center and right of the advance were the 163rd and 161st Brigades respectively. These troops were tasked with penetrating Turkish defenses at the Rafat salient until they reached Kefr Kasim before swinging east. The battle rested largely on how quickly the 54th Division could push through Turkish defenses and drive the Turkish defenders farther east to allow for the passage of British cavalry. Out of the necessity for speed to accomplish this task, the division carried little equipment with them. The troops left their haversacks behind and each took only two water bottles. Indeed, the soldiers dressed only in shorts and khaki jackets for swift movement despite the fact that they were to cross rocky terrain with wiry grass.[18] The rocky terrain, however, proved somewhat less of a problem owing to vigorous training between 14 September and 18 September for an advance over such territory. As a result of the training, one soldier commented that "I knew the ground better than many parts of my own parish."[19] This preparation served the division well in its crucial task.

The advance of the 54th Division began earlier than the others, at 3:50 AM before the artillery barrage, in lieu of the crucial need to open a hole in Turkish defenses as the hinge in the door described by Wavell. While the French detachment occupied Arara in the night of 19 September, the British crossed steep foothills in the region of Observatory Hill that rose 300 to 400 feet above ravines that intersected them. The British encountered little resistance in the drive to Kefr Kasim due to surprise being achieved over the Turks as their 77mm artillery fired high explosive rounds behind the advancing British owing to the rapidity of their movement. While British troops did encounter some stiff resistance at Crown Hill, one of the worst problems was the fact that elements of the division ended up in the zone of fire for the British artillery

---

17 Great Britain, Imperial War Museum, 8 October 1918 Letter of Blake O'Sullivan, O'Sullivan J.F.B. MSS 77/167/1, 3.
18 T. Gibbons, *With the 1/5th Essex in the East* (Colchester, UK: Benham, 1921), 141.
19 Gibbons, *With the 1/5th Essex in the East*, 141.

barrage. Water also became an issue very quickly as some elements of the division were short of it only a few hours after the beginning of the advance.[20] Even so, by late afternoon the 54th Division with the French enjoyed complete success in taking their objectives. By the end of the first day's operations the British captured 700 prisoners, nine artillery pieces, and 20 machine guns while suffering 535 casualties. At 3:45 p.m., while the division lay in the region of Sivri Tepe, Major General Hare received orders for a general chase of retreating Turkish troops north across the Wadi Kanah. Once in that area, Hare was to occupy the hills just north of the wadi.

The successful efforts of the infantry led to the ride of the Desert Mounted Corps through the penetrated Turkish defenses as the cavalry formed the crucial element for the Battle of Megiddo. The 4th and 5th divisions of the Desert Mounted Corps were given strict orders not to pursue any enemy units not directly in their line of advance.[21] These orders reflected the need of the cavalry to ride as quickly as possible to their objectives in order to encircle the retreating Ottoman armies and thus destroy them. Allenby desired that the two divisions reach their objectives within 24 hours to accomplish this end. The target of the 4th Cavalry under the command of Major General Sir G. de S. Barrow was Afule some 50 miles behind Ottoman lines. The plan called for Barrow to ride through the area of Turkish lines penetrated by the 7th Lahore Division and push for the Musmus Pass as it emptied into the Plain of Esdraelon since it was the only pass capable of supporting wheeled transport for logistical support. The 5th Cavalry under Major General H.J. Macandrew was tasked with reaching Beisan some 80 miles in the Turkish rear with its ride beginning in the area of Turkish defenses penetrated by the 60th Division. Macandrew would ride northward to Abu Shushe while in route to Beisan where he would send a detachment to Nazareth, the headquarters of Yildirim Army Group, in an attempt to not only seize the town but also capture General Liman von Sanders.

The 4th Cavalry left its bivouac in the region of Sarona between 4:00 AM and 4:30 AM. Attached to the division was also the Australian Mounted Division of Major General H.W. Hodgson, the 11th Light Armored Motor Battery, and one light car patrol. The brigades of the division moved forward to a position southeast of Jlil where they remained to water and feed the horses as British infantry pushed through Ottoman lines. At 8:40 AM, Barrow received permission to begin his march north through the Plain of Sharon with the 36th Jacobs Horse Regiment and three horse artillery batteries in the lead. None of the elements of the 4th Cavalry encountered any resistance from Ottoman troops in the region of their original defensive lines due to the success enjoyed by the infantry in accomplishing their mission. The first resistance from Ottoman defenders came as the 10th and 12th Cavalry Brigades

---

20   C.C.R. Murphy, *The History of the Suffolk Regiment, 1914-1927* (London: Hutchinson and Patterson, 1928), 316.
21   Great Britain, National Archives, "Instructions to General Officer Commanding Desert Mounted Corps", 9 September 1918, Diary of the General Headquarters Egyptian Expeditionary Force, WO 95/4371.

moved over marshes in the region of Iskanderune. Here they encountered only feeble attacks from the Ottoman Eighth Army's Depot Regiment as the Turks saw a wall of British cavalry advancing on their position. This caused the regiment to panic and attempt to flee, but they were run down by the 36th Jacobs Horse Regiment with 126 of the Turks being captured as prisoners of war. By 10:00 p.m. the 4th Cavalry lay at Hudeira with patrols reaching as far as the Musmus Pass. By this time Barrow had established a headquarters at Kerkur where the general urged his men to continue pressing forward. Once at his new headquarters, Barrow learned that Brigadier General Howard-Vyse in command of the 10th Cavalry Brigade had decided that he could not advance farther until after 11:30 p.m. in order to water his horses. Barrow told him to continue riding at 11:00 p.m. even if the horses were not fully watered for the sake of speed. He then rode to the farthest northern position of his division, occupied by the 2nd Lancers of the 10th Brigade, and told them to push through the Musmus Pass at 11:45 p.m. . The vital Musmus Pass has as its southern mouth the town of Musmus and extends along the Wadi Ara on the southern edge of the Samarian Hills with the northern mouth being El Lajjun, also known as Megiddo for which the battle is named.[22] At this point, the pass empties into the Plain of Esdraelon in a position where a person at Megiddo, lying three or four hundred feet above the plain, can see Nazareth as it is ten miles away with the center of the Plain of Esdraelon containing Afule. Barrow's ride to the 10th Brigade was fortuitous as he soon realized that the 10th Brigade, with ultimately the 11th Brigade following it, had mistakenly ridden ten miles north of the Musmus Pass. Barrow quickly reversed this potentially disastrous situation while relieving Captain D.S. Davison of the 2nd Lancers of his command as a consequence of the mistake.

 As the 4th Cavalry Division advanced so too did the 5th Cavalry Division. Major General H.J. Macandrew's forces were in their starting position at Arsuf on the coast of the Mediterranean. Attached to the force was 12th Light Armored Motor Battery and the 7th Light Car Patrol. At 7:00 AM Macandrew received permission to begin his advance north. The 5th Cavalry, with the 13th Brigade in the lead, encountered no Turkish resistance and by 11:00 AM took Liktera. R.H. Wilson in his memoirs described well the collapsed Turkish defense: "We over-took hundreds of bewildered Turks and Germans, still plodding along in the same direction we were going. We just waved to them…some just sat down and lit a cigarette and some even began preparing meals-but none offered any resistance.[23] Indeed, the British covered their first 25 miles so quickly that the cavalry exhausted their animals. The advance had been so fast that in the opening hours of the operation Macandrew, having appreciated its speed and the possible problem of tiring out the horses, tried unsuccessfully to reach the 13th Brigade and tell them to slow down the advance. His failure to reach the 13th Brigade in time led him to communicate to Chauvel that he did not intend to continue his

---

22 For more detail concerning the geography of the region, see Falls, 516.
23 Great Britain, Imperial War Museum, Wilson R.H. MSS 72/25/1, 52.

march north until 6:15 p.m. in order to take care of his horses.[24] Even so, the progress of the 5th Cavalry as well as the 4th in the opening stages of the campaign were a smashing success and a tribute to General Allenby's planning and the execution of it by his officers.

While the infantry of the XXI Corps and the Desert Mounted Corps formed the brunt of the British attack in the Battle of Megiddo, operations unfolded farther east in order to pressure Ottoman forces simultaneous to the main British offensive. To the east of XXI Corps lay XX Corps under the command of Lieutenant General Sir P.W. Chetwode. His corps comprised the 10th and 53rd divisions with a small detachment of a regiment and assorted smaller units, known as Watson's Force, lying in between them. The task of XX Corps was at first to mount a diversionary attack on the night of 18 September in order to play to Liman von Sanders' suspicions, and the British deception that the main attack was to unfold in the region of the Jordan Valley rather than on the coastline. By the night on 19 September, this heavy diversionary assault broke through Ottoman defenses at Sharon. From this point the corps had as its target a line from Aqrabe to Jemma that lay some seven miles north of the British point of advance. To accomplish this task Chetwode used the Nablus road. He had a great deal of the motorized transport of the Egyptian Expeditionary Force, being 180 vehicles as opposed to the 240 vehicles used by XXI Corps.[25] Unlike the general experience of the troops of XXI Corps, Chetwode's soldiers met concerted resistance from Turkish and German troops as they faced elements of the German Asia Korps and the Seventh Army of General Mustapha Kemal. Turkish and German positions were well dug in with the terrain consisting of rocky ridges. The stiffer resistance to the British was in part the result of the belief held by the high command of Yildirim that the British offensive would unfold in points around the Jordan Valley. Also, the fine Turkish defense was the result of Mustapha Kemal, who on the night of 18 September had been in telephone contact with his two corps commanders to order preparations to defend against a British assault.[26] Additionally, Allenby in his preparations for the massive assault on the coastline had stripped Chetwode's corps of much of its artillery. Throughout 19 September and into the early hours of 20 September there was very bloody fighting with only a halting British advance. Even so, while this defense was certainly a testimony to the fighting acumen of the Ottoman Seventh Army, it unfolded in a context where the Turkish resistance proved futile. While Mustapha Kemal conducted his defense the British Desert Mounted Corps was steadily sitting astride his lines of communication to the north.[27] This situation meant that the Seventh Army faced encirclement and destruction at the hands of the British.

---

24   Falls, *History of the Great War*, 523.
25   Falls, 458.
26   Lord Kinross, *Ataturk: A Biography of Mustapha Kemal, Father of Modern Turkey* (New York: William Morrow and Company, 1965.), 139.
27   H.S. Gullet, *The Official History of Australia in the War of 1914-1918*, Vol. 7, *Sinai and Palestine: The Australian Imperial Force in Sinai and Palestine, 1914-1918* (Sydney: Angus

Supplementing the offensive drives of the Egyptian Expeditionary Force was the fine work of the Palestinian Brigade of the Royal Air Force. On the first day of operations British aircraft dropped 11.25 tons of bombs and expended 66,000 rounds on the Ottoman defenders.[28] The 1st Squadron Australian Flying Corps conducted the majority of the strategic bombing of Turkish positions with its Handley Page bomber, DH9 aircraft, and Bristol fighters. This force bombed retreating Turkish units, attacking some 2,000 cavalry and 5,000 infantry around Et Tire as they retreated in the face of the British advance. These attacks not only depleted the retreating Turkish columns, but further British sorties damaged Ottoman logistics. On 19 September, two Bristol aircraft attacked a large column of trucks on the Wadi El Fara road.[29] While these attacks did not destroy the column, it did greatly slow their retreat while British cavalry rode to encircle them.

As these collective attacks unfolded, the last portion of the British line in the region of the Jordan Valley where the Ottomans thought the offensive would take place, saw virtually no British assaults. In this sector was Chaytor's Force, under the command of Major General Sir E.W.C. Chaytor who was assigned the defense of the British right flank from the northern end of the Dead Sea to a point eight miles northwest of Jericho. The defensive orders for Chaytor were not only the product of the crux of the battle being far to the west on the coast, but also that his force was of questionable offensive value. Chaytor's command was a ragtag group of two battalions of British West Indians, two battalions of Jews raised mainly in England, the 20th Indian Infantry Brigade, and the ANZAC Mounted Division. The latter unit was wholly unfit for duty because it had guarded the area of the Jordan Valley during the terrible heat of the summer months and was therefore exhausted and many troops were ill. Since Allenby assigned him a defensive role, Chaytor did what he could to improve his position through the construction of defensive works. These included the construction of stone works in some areas of his front, the expansion of trench systems, and the erection of wire to impede enemy attacks.[30] These measures proved wise not only due to the condition of his force, but also since Turkish strength in the area, being primarily the Ottoman Fourth Army, was strong owing to the Ottoman belief that an attack would unfold in that sector. Further operations for Chaytor depended on the success of the British in the main area of the assault. If the British achieved success at the coast, there was a good possibility that the Ottoman Fourth Army would retreat up the Hejaz railroad bound for Deraa. If this occurred, Chaytor could harass the enemy's retreat and capture the Jordan River crossing at Jisr ed Damiye. No

---

and Robertson, 1923), 701.
28 Great Britain, National Archives, Diary of General Headquarters Egyptian Expeditionary Force, 19 September 1918, WO 95/4371.
29 Gullet, 153.
30 Australian War Memorial, Diary of the 1st Australian Light Horse Brigade, 1 September 1918, AWM 4 10/1/50.

operations, however, occurred on 19 September as the enemy continued to hold strong positions north of Chaytor's line.

The lack of operations on the eastern British line, however, belied the smashing blow of the British to Turkish defenses on the first day of the Battle of Megiddo. Indeed, the Turks lost the battle on the first day owing to the destruction of their front-line defensive works farther west. British soldier W.G. Mead described the carnage as he inspected the Turkish front line trench following the British assault:

> Being inquisitive, what I saw after an artillery bombardment and a Lancer charge I have to relate despite it being unpleasant writing or reading. Harold Major was my companion and we dropped down into the Turkish front line trench and walked until we stopped dead in our tracks facing the dead. Turkish soldiers remained propped against a parapet, blasted to death. Passing along and into another bay of the trench, evidently where our infantry dropped in, we saw two soldiers skewered together against the wall and who had died as the result of a simultaneous bayonet thrust. I had had enough-the sight shocked and revolted me but more was to come. Later on I saw Turkish soldiers laying on their stomachs having been caught on the run and lanced through the back, to be shaken off the end of the lance, there to lay flat on their face in death. There too was a German gunner, still seated beside his gun having been blasted to death. A German trumpeter lay flat on his face with several bullet holes-from machine gun fire-straddled across his back.[31]

Captured Turkish and German officers and troops provided similar accounts of what can only be termed a rout of Turkish and German forces. The rapidity of the advance and the preponderance of British force were the cause. Captured Turkish and German soldiers and officers particularly highlighted the speed of the attack. A British intelligence officer related information from a captured Turkish officer that described the situation of the Eighth Army and the German Asia Korps, being the forces on which the main British blow fell:

> On 19th September the 7th and 19th divisions [Ottoman Eighth Army and German Asia Korps respectively] broke down at 0430. The 20th Division [Ottoman Eighth Army] was thus surrounded and broken up by about 0500. The reason for the Turkish debacle was mainly the unexpected rapidity with which our infantry broke up the 20th Division which was regarded as the best in the Turkish Army.[32]

---

31 Great Britain Imperial War Museum, W.G. Mead MSS PP/MCR/7, 93-94.
32 Great Britain, National Archives, Diary of GHQ Intelligence, September 1918, WO 157/731.

The situation for General Sanders is also indicative of the speed of the assault. In keeping with the communication problems between Yildirim General Headquarters and the front and owing to the speed of the British, it was only several days after the initial British assault that Sanders fully grasped the fact that the Eighth Army and German Asia Korps were in a state of total collapse with the exception of the 16th Division of the latter. Sanders claimed in his memoirs that communication with Eighth Army ceased about 0700 on 19 September.[33] The destruction of the Ottoman Eighth Army's defense was the primary reason for British success in the Battle of Megiddo. The virtual destruction of the army left the coastal flank of the Turks exposed and the Seventh and eventually Fourth armies in danger of encirclement, which was exactly Allenby's plan. This situation was not only the result of the cavalry, but the efforts of British infantry that made the cavalry advance possible.

While Sanders was largely oblivious to the dire situation of the Eighth Army, the commanders on the ground were fully aware not only of their situation, but the disaster that it foretold for the entire Turkish defense of Palestine. General Djevad Pasha, commander of Eighth Army, knew the extent of the disaster by 0850 as he attempted to send a report to Sanders on the situation, which may not have ever reached Yildirim General Headquarters. Djevad Pasha wrote "I am in great difficulty because of the terrible situation on the right wing...The enemy has broken through our lines in spite of our counter-attacks...Without assistance operations are impossible.[34] Subordinates of Djevad Pasha also were well aware of the gravity of the situation as from the Eighth Army Headquarters at Tul Karm all could see the massed cavalry of the British Desert Mounted Corps, with their swords and lances glinting in the morning sun, riding north through the Plain of Sharon. Many Turkish and German forces on the Ottoman coastal flank by the night of 19 September were in wholesale retreat with 10,000 soldiers withdrawing on the road towards Jenin. The mass confusion of the Eighth Army is evidenced by the fact that Colonel Refet Bey, the commander of XXII Corps of the Eighth Army, became completely cut off from his forces. Refet Bey, two of his orderlies, and his aide-de-camp spent a week alone as they attempted their retreat. Not only was the retreat itself a disaster, but all of the withdrawing troops were under threat of capture by British forces thanks to the encirclement of the operation and particularly the intelligence of their movements afforded by the British Royal Air Force.

Such intelligence allowed Allenby to press his advantage on 20 September with a resumption of the northern advance of his infantry, particularly through operations of the XXI Corps. While the 5th Australian Light Horse Brigade of the Australian Mounted Division, Desert Mounted Corps, advanced from Tul Karm towards Aije north of Sebustiye to cut Turkish railroad communications, which they accomplished through the use of explosives, the 3rd Indian Lahore Division resumed their drive at

---

33 Edward Erickson, *Ottoman Army Effectiveness in World War I*, 148-149.
34 Erickson, *Ottoman Army Effectiveness in World War I*, 148.

5:00 AM. Their task was to take Azzun held by elements of the German Asia Korps. German resistance ceased in the area after 12:30 p.m. and by the close of the day 8th Brigade lay at Jinsafut while the 9th Brigade bivouacked at Kufr Qaddum.

This success was not one mirrored by the 7th Indian Meerut Division. Its experience is indicative of the problems posed by logistics behind enemy lines. Lack of sufficient water was a particular challenge for Major-General Fane, who felt compelled to slow portions of his advance owing to the exhaustion of his troops from lack of water. So dire was the situation that by 22 September Fane met with his officers to discuss the situation and stress the importance of water discipline among the men. The day before, Fane requested of corps commander Bulfin that exact boundaries of operation be set between the 7th Division and those divisions adjacent in order to conserve existing water supplies in Fane's area of operations.[35] An exception to the division's halting advance on 20 September was that of the 19th Brigade that came under fire at 11:00 AM at the village of Beit Lid. The objective of the brigade, in keeping with the need to address the problem of water supply, was El Masudiye railroad station as that area had available supplies. Brigadier General Weir's brigade, however, had not had any water since 5:00 AM and was exhausted in the face of well entrenched Turks in houses and among cactus that put up a stiff resistance through machine gun fire. Only at 5:30 p.m. did El Masudiye station fall to the British while the original time table for the advance called for its seizure around 2:00 p.m. . While successful, the attack on El Masudiye exhibited that British operations were beginning to suffer minor setbacks through insufficient logistical support.

Finally, 20 September saw action for the 60th Division, but this was rather limited owing to the position of the force. As the division primarily tasked with the destruction of Ottoman forces on the coastline in order to open the gap for the advance of the Desert Mounted Corps, there were few Turks left in their sector due to their wholesale retreat. The 179th Brigade marched to Tul Karm and then deployed against Anebta, which it took at 11:20 AM. This brigade secured the railroad tunnel there pursuant to the orders to all corps commanders to seize as much of the enemy's logistical and communication network as possible for use of the Egyptian Expeditionary Force. While the 179th Brigade secured Anebta, the 181st Brigade took up a position north of the Tul Karm-Anebta road.

While XXI Corps continued its advance north so too did the XX Corps that was assigned the task of driving enemy forces around Mount Ephraim back towards the British cavalry that progressively encircled them in the rear. Progress for the 53rd Division proved slow in part due to logistical problems that also plagued elements of XXI Corps, but also from Turkish resistance. The 160th Brigade stormed Jibeit at 4:40 AM using a bayonet charge only to be counter-attacked at 8:00 AM by a battalion of the 109th Turkish Regiment, which was part of the Ottoman Seventh Army. The British only recaptured the area at 12:45 p.m. through an artillery bombardment. The

---

35 Gullet, 704.

159th Brigade proved somewhat more successful by taking the village of Ras Et Tawil at 3:00 AM. The halting advance of the 158th Brigade mirrored that of the 160th Brigade, which slowed due to work being conducted on the Forth Wadi Road in order to bring up more supplies.

Progress for the 10th Division was also halting, but primarily due to Ottoman defenses rather than logistics. Units of the 10th Division encountered a new enemy defensive line that lay between Iskaka and Kefar Haris. This new line contained not only a large number of machine gun units, but also three or four batteries of artillery. Even so, by night fall the division held both Ikaka and Kefar Haris, due in part to the attack of the 54th Sikh Regiment that breached the center of the Ottoman line. At 11:30 p.m., the division then marched north with its target being the headquarters of the Ottoman Seventh Army at Nablus. Turkish resistance also collapsed as news reached Turkish commanders that the Desert Mounted Corps had reached Afule and Beisan, thus increasingly cutting off avenues of retreat for the Ottoman Seventh Army. Mustapha Kemal consequently embarked on a fighting retreat in an atmosphere where he had only three avenues of escape from the region of Nablus to that of the Jordan Valley: through Majdal Beni Fadl, an old Roman road that ran through Beik Furik, and the road from Nablus to the Wadi El Fara that led to Jist et Damiye. Chetwode, in command of XX Corps, knew the situation of the Turks well and resolved to press his advance to drive the Turks back towards the Desert Mounted Corps. At 6:30 p.m. he ordered the 53rd Division to march for the Wadi El Fara Road while the 10th Division was tasked with an advance on Nablus. These orders came despite the fatigue of his men as the situation demanded swift action as part of the destruction of Ottoman forces through encirclement.

The threat of being trapped by the Desert Mounted Corps became a very real possibility on 20 September for the Ottomans and Germans as the corps continued its advance north and west. Owing to the prior navigational error of the 10th Brigade, Barrow chose, in the early morning hours, to continue the ride of his 4th Cavalry Division with the 12th Brigade in the lead followed by most of the 10th Brigade, accompanied by the 11th Light Armored Car Battery, through the Musmus Pass into the Plain of Esdraelon. It was the 2nd Lancers Regiment that encountered what Turkish defense there was at the Musmus Pass. This unit at 5:30 AM discovered the Turkish 13th Depot Regiment with orders to guard the hills overlooking the pass, but as they had not reached it in time the Turks chose to set up defensive positions in the plain at El Lajjun, or Megiddo. The ruins of this ancient town lay at the northern mouth of the Musmus Pass. What followed was the engagement that garnered the name of Allenby's operation, being the Battle of Megiddo. Captain D.S. Davison, in command of the 2nd Lancers, ordered the armored cars of the 11th Light Armored Car Battery to engage the enemy in a frontal assault with a squadron of the regiment in support. Davison then took the other two squadrons of his regiment and used one each to mount charges on the flanks of the Turks. The ensuing panic as Davison's lancers ran down the Turks resulted in the Ottoman soldiers firing too high to hit Davison's men. In the space of five minutes, 46 Turks were speared by British lances while another 470 surrendered. This victory came at a cost of only one lancer and 12 horses as casualties.[36] The engagement is indicative of the value of cavalry and armored cars against infantry as the Turks had not time to react to the speed of the British assault.

The victory against the Turks at Megiddo allowed for the passage of the Desert Mounted Corps into the Plain of Esdraelon for an advance on Afule. By 7:45 AM, elements of the 4th Division approached the town with Captain Davison's 2nd Lancers in the lead. As they approached, Davison could see "streams of lorries...moving out along the Beisan Road."[37] While this might suggest that the Turks were abandoning the defense of the town, this proved incorrect. Davison's force came under fire from the Turks at a range of half a mile. By the time that the 2nd Lancers approached the outskirts of the town, Davison found that resistance had ceased since the 20th Deccan Horse Regiment of the 5th Cavalry Division had taken Afule. At the same time, the 34th Poona Regiment of the same division was in possession of the road to Nazareth. The fall of Afule resulted in the capture of 75 Germans and 200 Turks. Also seized were ten locomotives, 50 trucks, and three airplanes. In terms of the latter, the number became four aircraft lost since soon after the fall of Afule a pilot landed his aircraft there in the belief that the Ottomans still held the town. When he realized his mistake, the pilot attempted to take off again only to be shot down and the machine taken intact.[38] The Turks also lost the trucks that attempted to flee to Beisan as they were run down by the armored cars of the British.

With the Turkish railroad lines south and east of Afule cut, Barrow ordered the 4th Cavalry Division at 1:00 p.m. to ride over the 16 miles that separated Afule from Beisan, being originally the target of the 5th Cavalry Division. The 19th Lancers Regiment of the 12th Cavalry Brigade remained to garrison Afule. As the division rode down the path of the railroad line to Beisan, it encountered the first of the torrent of Turkish and German troops that had been pushed north from their defensive lines by British infantry. These men were quickly made prisoners of war. Beisan itself fell after little opposition with some 100 Turkish soldiers captured along with three howitzers. As a further testimony of the total surprise of the Turks in the face of the rapid British assault on their positions, these howitzers faced east rather than to the northwest, being the direction of the British assault. During the night, the British captured an additional 700 Turks retreating north as the encirclement of Ottoman troops began to unfold in earnest.[39] The 4th Cavalry with the fall of Beisan ceased

---

36 Great Britain, National Archives, Diary of 7th Division General Headquarters, 21-22 September, WO 95/4704.
37 Great Britain, National Archives, Diary of 4th Cavalry Division General Staff, Report of Captain Davison, WO 95/4510.
38 R.M.P. Preston, *The Desert Mounted Corps: An Account of the Cavalry Operations in Palestine and Syria, 1917-1918* (New York: Houghton Mifflin, 1923), 210. See also Falls, 520.
39 Great Britain, National Archives, Diary of 4th Cavalry Division General Staff, WO 95/4510.

operations as all objectives were met for the day. Over the course of 34 hours since the beginning of the ride through the Plain of Sharon, the division had covered 80 miles. Further operations were not possible since the horses of the division needed to recover and the division's supply train lay 50 miles away from Beisan. No trucks were able to deliver supplies for the division until 21 September.

As operations unfolded for the 4th Cavalry, 1:00 AM on 20 September saw the 5th Cavalry Division reaching the village of Jara with the vanguard of the division being the 13th Brigade under Brigadier General P.J.V. Kelly. Kelly, who had 10 years of experience in the Egyptian cavalry prior to the war, spoke fluent Arabic. He led the division in the hopes that his knowledge could help to garner intelligence from local inhabitants concerning the area of advance.[40] The 14th Brigade subsequently joined the 13th Brigade for a march through the hills between Jara and the next objective, being the village of Abu Shushe. This village fell to the British at 2:15 AM as the division prepared to march on the headquarters of Yildirim Army Group at Nazareth. The ride to Nazareth proved torturous as the British had to ride single file through the hills. The path that they took could hardly be called a road as it was virtually indistinguishable from the surrounding terrain in the moonlit night. In addition, much of the path consisted of rocky formations: "We kept losing sight of the man in the front, as the way was over sheer rocky mountain. Several times we had to remove packs from the machine gun pack horses to squeeze them through the cracks in the rocks."[41] By 4:30 AM, despite the challenge of the march, the division found itself on the outskirts of Nazareth with orders to not only seize the city but, if possible, General Liman von Sanders himself.

Unfortunately for the British, however, the endeavor to capture the commander of Yildirim Army Group suffered from little information of the layout of the city and which exact structure was the headquarters of Sanders' command. All the British knew was that Sanders' general headquarters lay next to a large truck depot. Riding first into the city in search of Sanders was the I/1st Gloucester Yeomanry Regiment. The regiment reached the heart of the town, specifically the Hotel Germania where many of Yildirim's staff lived but fighting in the narrow streets of the city began in short order with British cavalry reaching a point only 200 yards from Sanders' headquarters. From there the British had to withdraw from Nazareth at 10:55 AM owing to insufficient support and heavy machine gun fire from buildings.[42] Only the 13th Brigade mounted the assault on Nazareth as the exhaustion of the horses in the 14th Brigade precluded their involvement. One cavalryman of the brigade that searched for Sanders illustrates the frustration of the British over the missed opportunity: "I

---

40 Preston, 206.
41 Great Britain, Imperial War Museum, R.H. Wilson MSS 82/25/1, 53-54.
42 Great Britain, Imperial War Museum, A.C. Alan-Williams MSS AC 74/55/1A, 3.

realized that my hopes of going down in history as the man who caught a Commander-in-Chief were ruined....it had all been a waste of time."[43]

While the initial attempt to seize Nazareth failed as well as the attempt to capture Sanders, the first assault on the city did have military value. The disruption caused by the attack on Sanders' headquarters forced its evacuation. As a result, any potential command and control of Yildirim from Nazareth was ruined although owing to prior communication difficulties at the outset of the British operation that had already occurred. Sanders left Nazareth at 1:15 p.m. bound north for Tiberias which would be as his new headquarters. According to his housekeeper, who the British subsequently captured and interrogated, Sanders at the opening of the British assault had dashed down the stairs of his quarters while still in his pajamas.[44] Ultimately, he was able to successfully flee in his staff car because the road leading from Nazareth north to Tiberias was still open. Despite the failure to capture Sanders or capture Nazareth in the initial attack, a subsequent assault led to the fall of the city to British cavalry.

While the 4th and 5th Cavalry throughout 19-20 September conducted their crucial operations to encircle the Turks, the third division of the Desert Mounted Corps, the Australian Mounted Division under the command of Major General H.W. Hodgson, saw little action on the first day of the battle. This division served as the reserve of the Desert Mounted Corps and camped on the night of 19 September on the right bank of the Nahr Iskanderune in the Plain of Sharon, being well behind the advancing other two divisions. From that location the 3rd Light Horse brigade of the division set out at 1:00 AM on 20 September for Megiddo where at noon that day Chauvel established his advanced headquarters there. Once established at Megiddo, Chauvel relied on elements of the light horse for communication with the 4th and 5th Cavalry divisions, as the speed of their advance precluded the large-scale use of wireless transmissions.

The involvement of the Australian Mounted Division in the Battle of Megiddo truly began after 2:45 p.m. on 20 September when Chauvel received a report detailing the retreat of large numbers of Turks and Germans towards Jenin nine miles southeast of Megiddo. Chauvel subsequently ordered the 3rd Light Horse Brigade of Brigadier General L.C. Wilson to march on Jenin and occupy it in order to lay in wait for the retreating enemy forces. Wilson rode for his objective at 4:30 p.m. with the 11th Light Armored Motor Battery and the 19th Brigade Royal Horse drawn Artillery in support. At the head of the formation was the 10th Light Horse regiment with six machine guns that proceeded at a gallop to get to Jenin ahead of the retreating Ottomans and Germans. The subsequent capture of Jenin, with little concerted resistance, proved a disaster for the Ottomans as 10,000 Turks and Germans were in retreat to the town. These troops were first attacked by Royal Air Force planes that dropped 40 bombs and fired 4,000 rounds into the massed columns of retreating soldiers between Burka

---

43 Great Britain, Imperial War Museum, A.C. Alan-Williams MSS AC 74/55/1A, 58.
44 Great Britain, Imperial War Museum, "The Peregrinations of Private Powell", E.S. Powell MSS PP/MCR/37, 135.

northbound for Jenin.[45] Shortly before sunset these same troops encountered elements of the 3rd Cavalry Brigade. Indicative of the terrible morale of the Ottomans and Germans at this point was the situation found by the 23 riders of the 10th Regiment of the brigade. As night fell the cavalrymen could make out a large column travelling up the road to Jenin, although they were unsure of their number. On the suggestion of Trooper T.B. George to his commanding officer Lieutenant R.R.W. Patterson, the regiment fired into the air in an attempt to compel the enemy force to surrender. Since it was dark, the hope was that they would be unaware of the number of British cavalry. Patterson ended up negotiating with a German nurse who knew English with the result being the surrender of 2,800 soldiers and four artillery pieces to a party of 23 Australian cavalrymen. By the morning, the number of prisoners of war had swollen to 8,000 soldiers in an environment where an ammunition depot in Jenin burned and Arab locals looted the town.[46] The fall of Jenin proved crushing for Ottoman fortunes. Not only did the Ottomans and Germans lose thousands of soldiers, but in terms of logistics the loss of the town cut communications and one of the few avenues of retreat north that remained. In addition, the town had workshops, three hospitals, and an aerodrome. Also captured at Jenin were 20,000 British pounds sterling in gold.[47]

The end of 20 September presented a situation where the British accomplished all of the initial objectives for the Battle of Megiddo in those areas west of the Jordan Valley. British cavalry sat astride all the major lines of retreat for those Turks and Germans that fled from their initial defensive positions at the opening of the engagement. The largescale capture of Ottoman and German troops bound for Jenin only proved the first of several episodes where the Ottomans lost masses of men and material not to engagements, but to the success of Allenby's plan of encirclement as the Ottomans had no way to exit the area of southern Palestine.

A great deal of the British work of capturing retreating Ottomans and Germans occurred on 21 September, the last day of concerted operations by the infantry of the Egyptian Expeditionary Force. The XXI Corps continued to advance north while the 3rd Indian Lahore Division continued their advance at 5:00 a.m., meeting with little opposition. The end of its day's march found the division occupying a defensive line that ran five and half miles between Rafidia to a point just east of Burqa. Meanwhile the 7th Division in the region of El Masudiye Station captured 400 wounded Turks and Germans. By the end of the day, the division took an additional 600 prisoners of war that were largely sick in hospital at Sebastiye, which the division also conquered.[48] Additionally in the same operational area of the 7th Division lay the 5th Australian Light Horse Regiment, detached from the Australian and New Zealand Mounted

---

45   F.M. Cutlack, *The Official History of Australia in the War of 1914-1918*. Volume 8. *The Australian Flying Corps in the Western and Eastern Theaters of War, 1914-1918* (Sydney, Australia: Angus and Robertson, 1923.), 156.
46   Gullet, 707-708.
47   Preston, 215.
48   Falls, *History of the Great* War, 509.

Division of Chaytor's Force. This force seized Nablus, the former headquarters of the Ottoman Seventh Army, with little resistance since the Ottomans had already retreated north. By the close of the day, operations were largely over for the XXI Corps in the Battle of Megiddo. The exception was the 60th Division on the coast that ended its advance on 23 September at Iktabi-Shuweikeh-Kakon-Burin. Casualties for the corps were relatively light; they had 3,378 of which only 446 died. Of those killed in action were 195 British dead and 217 Indian troops.[49] In return, the corps achieved the destruction of the Ottoman Eighth Army that made the cavalry encirclement of the Ottomans and Germans possible.

The day of 21 September also saw the end of concerted action of the XX Corps as its divisions continued to advance north. Like the XXI Corps, the divisions of XX Corps met little resistance due to the wholesale retreat of the Ottomans and Germans. The 53rd Division to the far east of the British line of attack occupied Birket el Qusr at 1:00 a.m. before taking Majdal Beni Fadl near dawn with little opposition. The target of the division for the day was the town of Aqurabe, which also fell with little fighting in a situation where Chetwode considered a further advance to Wadi Al Fara. Chetwode, however, halted the division at Aqurabe since there was no need to advance farther. By the time the division reached Aqurabe the section of road between Nablus and Ain es Subian on the Wadi Al Fara road, being a line of retreat for the Ottoman Seventh Army, was under British artillery fire while a further portion of the road was under assault by the Royal Air Force. Overall, operations for the 53rd Division had cost 690 casualties in return for the capture of 1,195 prisoners of war and nine artillery pieces.

Whilst the 53rd Division pushed towards Aqurabe, the 10th Division continued its drive towards Nablus. the former headquarters of the Ottoman Seventh Army. This town, like so many others for the British on this day of operations had fallen with scant resistance. Indeed, the town was already under British control upon the arrival of the 10th Division. By the end of the day, the division had covered a total of 20 miles of poor terrain overall during the operation with only six hours of uninterrupted sleep and suffered only three officers and 103 soldiers killed. The division also counted additionally seventeen officers and 683 soldiers as wounded. In return, the division took all of its objectives in addition to taking 1,223 enemy combatants prisoner.[50]

While the 10th Division largely halted in Nablus, a contingent of the division's soldiers marched northeast towards Nabi Belan with the intention of blocking a portion of the Wadi Al Fara Road against the retreating elements of the Ottoman Seventh Army. This move, however, proved unnecessary since British officers found that two miles of the road were blocked with debris caused by the disaster suffered by the Ottomans retreating on the Wadi Al Fara Road from concerted attacks by the

---

49   Falls, 511.
50   James Kitchen, "The Indianization of the Egyptian Expeditionary Force: Palestine 1918", in Kaushik Roy, ed., *The Indian Army in the Two World Wars* (Boston: Brill, 2012), 187.

Royal Air Force. This attack began at 6:30 a.m. on 21 September as aircraft of the Palestine Brigade found a column of Seventh Army soldiers retreating up the Wadi Al Fara Road. The geography of this road rendered the Turks entirely vulnerable to attack from the air. On one side of the road lay a deep gorge that led down to the bed of the wadi whereas the other side was a steep stony bank. This gave the Turks no room to maneuver or seek cover from airstrikes. The attack began with two Australian aircraft attacking the lead elements of the column and scoring five direct hits with bombs whilst discharging 600 machine gun rounds into the retreating formation.[51] The damage inflicted to the lead of the Turkish column forced the rest to stop in an attempt to try and clear the wreckage from the road during which the Turks suffered additional attacks. An additional nine tons of bombs were dropped by the British and they expended an additional 56,000 machine gun rounds.[52] Whilst the attack resulted in few Turkish casualties, it produced mayhem and destruction along seven miles of the road, which further demoralized the retreating forces of Seventh Army. Amongst the wreckage were 100 artillery pieces, 55 trucks, 932 wagons, and 92 carts.[53] The attacks also completely dispersed the Turkish soldiers as they fled into the hills surrounding the wadi. According to one soldier "as far as the eye could reach, it [the Wadi Al Fara Road] was blocked by guns, wagons, and motor lorries. Many had fallen over the precipice and lay shattered in the wadi bed. Dead or wounded animals lay thick between the wagons and added to an indescribable tangle."[54] The destroyed vehicles took days for the British to clear in order to make the road operational. The assault not only created more chaos for the encircled forces of the Turks. It was also the first time in history that a major formation of infantry was destroyed by air power alone.[55] Finally, the attack serves as an illustration of General Edmund Allenby's penchant for using combined arms to accomplish the goals of his operation.

The infantry of the Egyptian Expeditionary Force, in concert with the Royal Air Force during their operations on 21 September, continued to push elements of the Yildirim Army Group north into the path of the cavalry of the Desert Mounted Corps. By this date, Allenby's cavalry had completely encircled the retreating forces of both Ottoman Seventh and Eighth armies. The result was that throughout 21-22 September the Desert Mounted Corps took so many prisoners that it nearly overwhelmed the corp's ability to effectively take charge of them all. While the 5th Cavalry

---

51   Cutlack, 160-161.
52   David R. Woodward, *Hell in the Holy Land: World War I in the Middle East* (Lexington, KY: University Press of Kentucky, 2006), 197. See also Great Britain, National Archives, Diary of General Headquarters Egyptian Expeditionary Force, 21 September 1918, WO 95/4371.
53   Cyril Falls, *Armageddon, 1918* (London: Weidenfeld and Nicolson, 1964), 79. See also H. Pirie Gordon, *A Brief Record of the Advance of the Egyptian Expeditionary Force* (London, HMSO: 1919), 113.
54   Great Britain, Imperial War Museum, Lord Hampton MSS DS/MISC/82, 80.
55   Bryan Perrett, *Megiddo 1918: Lawrence, Allenby, and the March on Damascus* (Westport, Conn.: Praeger, 2004), 58.

Division was at Nazareth, the 4th piqueting the Beisan-Afule road from the Jordan Valley to the Shatta Station with the aim of capturing the Yildirim soldiers that fled on the Wadi Al Fara Road. The position of the 4th Cavalry Division proved devastating for the Ottomans as, throughout the night of 21 September and the following day, the 4th Cavalry Division captured 4,000 prisoners of war as they marched towards Beisan and blundered into the British. These troops proved so fatigued and demoralized that they surrendered not only without a fight, but without being challenged by the British. The numbers captured by the 4th Cavalry Division only added to a colossal number of prisoners of war taken by the Egyptian Expeditionary Force. By 21 September, even before all 4,000 of those Yildirim forces marching to Beisan were in British hands, some 25,000 Ottoman and German prisoners of war were in British hands with the Ottoman Seventh and Eighth armies being consequently destroyed.

The only relatively intact force that remained of the Ottoman defenses west of the Jordan Valley was the German Asia Korps. Colonel von Oppen in the morning of 21 September had orders to support the retreat of the Ottoman Seventh Army but refused to obey the order. Instead, he reorganized his remaining force. The remnants of the 702nd and 703rd battalions were reformed into one new battalion while the 16th and 19th divisions as well as the 701st Battalion and a cavalry squadron remained intact. He then endeavored to retreat northward up the Wadi Al Fara Road, but at 10:00 a.m. learned of the disaster suffered by the Turkish column on that road at the hands of the Royal Air Force. The colonel then attempted to retreat via Beit Dejan southeast of Nablus to the Jordan at Jisr ed Damiye, but found his advance cut off by elements of the British XX Corps. At this point, he ordered a retreat north over Mount Ebal. While this avenue resulted in the loss of almost all of Oppen's artillery and supplies, his forces by the end of the day found themselves safely at Tammun to the north of the Wadi Al Fara Road having escaped British forces. Even so, Oppen bivouacked at Tammun without knowledge of the fact that the British were in occupation of Beisan north of his position.

Oppen's survival, however, could not reverse the complete disaster for the Ottomans. The loss of the Ottoman Seventh and Eighth armies proved a completely untenable situation for the Ottoman defense of Palestine. General Sanders in the morning of 21 September became increasingly aware of the debacle as he fled Nazareth by staff car to Samakh railroad station at the southern tip of the Sea of Galilee with the intention of establishing a new defensive line. Once in Samakh, Sanders rode by train to Deraa to contact the Ottoman Fourth Army, being the only intact Yildirim force remaining in the theater. That situation, however, was one that did not remain true as the next days unfolded.

The state of affairs that led to the deterioration of the Ottoman Seventh Army, commanded by General Mohammed Djemal Kucuk, resulted from the destruction of the Ottoman armies to his army's west that forced his withdrawal. This included an advance by Major General Sir E.W.C. Chaytor's Force in the Jordan Valley and attacks by the Arab allies of the British. Between 19-21 September, the Ottoman Fourth Army maintained pressure on Chaytor's Force as the general conducted a limited advance.

That strategy changed with intelligence that the Ottoman Seventh and Eighth armies were totally destroyed and the railway junction of Deraa was threatened by British cavalry moving through the Plain of Esdraelon. General Kucek thus saw his position as untenable. If the British conquered Deraa, his army would potentially suffer the same fate as the other two Ottoman armies farther west since the British would be in his rear. Kucek as a result ordered on 22 September a general retreat to Es Salt and Amman before retiring farther north to Damascus, Syria. Chaytor, around the same time, received orders to make a strong advance on Turkish positions in the Jordan Valley. Like British units farther west after the initial penetration of Turkish defenses, Chaytor's Force encountered little stiff resistance as the Ottomans focused on retreat. On 22 September, Chaytor's Force captured Jisr Ed Damiye, being a crossing point over the Jordan River and the last enemy defense west of that river. Further advances east towards Es Salt and Amman the following day clearly exhibited that the Turks were in wholesale retreat, destroying what they could not take with them: "A great column of smoke is rising from the hills in the direction of Shunet Nimrin. The enemy is burning his dumps."[56] As Chaytor's Force continued east it progressively encountered signs of the retreating Turks including blown bridges, abandoned ammunition dumps, and stores of sundry supplies. As part of the abandoned equipment, the British found a naval artillery piece they called "Jericho Jane" dumped in the Wadi Shumrin. This gun had been a source of distress for the British when the 4th Cavalry Division was headquartered at Gilgal Hotel in Jericho before the Battle of Megiddo. Major General Barrow, commander of the division, recalled one episode when "Jericho Jane" shelled his headquarters: "One shell caught the corner of the hotel close to my room. I hopped out of the bath and went through the drying process quicker than I had ever done, or shall, again."[57] The gun gained such notoriety that other commanders in the Egyptian Expeditionary Force commented on it as well. In June 1918 Barrow had visited Major General Shea in command of the 60th Division at Jerusalem when the town came under artillery fire. This prompted Lieutenant General Chetwode of XX Corps to write to Barrow: "For God's sake go back to Jericho; that gun follows you wherever you are."[58] Surely seeing the gun in the bottom of the Wadi Shumrin was a welcoming sight as Chaytor's Force advanced east. Indeed, it was also a sign of the collapsed defense of the Ottomans and Germans in Palestine.

The encounter with "Jericho Jane" came amidst the continuing decline in the fortunes of the Ottoman Fourth Army. The town of Amman fell to the British on 25 September in an attack by the 2nd Australian Light Horse Brigade and the New Zealand Mounted Rifles Brigade of Chaytor's Force. The Turks evacuated the town rather quickly with conditions there revealing further the extent of the Ottoman collapse:

---

56 Robert H. Goodsall, *Palestine Memories* (Canterbury, UK: Cross and Jackman, 1925), 176.
57 George de S. Barrow, *The Fire of Life* (London: Hutchinson, 1942), 190.
58 Barrow, 191.

> The Turks had evacuated the town in so great a hurry that they left behind a considerable quantity of stores, grain, and fodder, and most of their wounded. The bodies of numerous dead Turks lay about in the streets, and also the carcasses of a large number of animals. The whole place was in an indescribably filthy condition, and it was some days before the streets were cleaned up. A considerable number of prisoners were collected in the town, waiting to be evacuated to the prison camps in Palestine and Egypt, and the more robust of these were put to the work of burying the dead and otherwise cleaning up the streets. The wounded had been left in a shockingly bad state…there were no proper sanitary arrangements, and before our medical services had time to deal with the situation, a number of men died from sheer neglect.[59]

The loss of Amman proved a dire blow to the Ottoman retreat. It was a railway junction of the Hejaz railroad, meaning that any retreating Ottoman units south of Amman were cut off from logistical support and encircled by British troops. In addition, Amman was the only reliable source of water in the region. By the fall of Amman, the rear guard of the Ottoman Fourth Army lay trapped in the desert to the south of the town with no supply.

The result was the capture of the rearguard of the Fourth Army, which included 6,000 troops of the II Corps under the command of General Ali Bey Wahaby. This was the last major operation of Chaytor's Force in the Battle of Megiddo. On 27 September a Turkish prisoner of war informed the British of this body of soldiers whereupon a British aircraft dropped a message to the retreating Turks that unless they surrendered by 9:00 a.m. the following morning they would be subjected to bombing attacks. The message also pointed out that surrender was the only option as all water sources north lay in the hands of Chaytor's Force.[60]

While Wahaby agreed to negotiations he refused to lay down his arms. By 29 September, there was a problem concerning the surrender as the Turks found themselves surrounded by Arabs of the Beni Sakr tribe. These Arabs were enemies of the Ottomans and had followed Wahaby's retreat. The Australian official history of the war in Palestine and Syria placed the number of these horse-backed Arabs at upwards of 10,000 men.[61] The situation became so dire as to prompt Chaytor himself to travel to the scene at Kastal 16 miles south of Amman by motor car while the 2nd Australian Light Horse Brigade formed a cordon around the Turks to allow their surrender. Due to the relatively small size of the brigade, however, the British elected to allow the Turks to keep their armaments while translators attempted to reason with the Arabs.[62] Throughout the night, the Australians and Turks bivouacked with one another, eating

---

59 Goodsall, 184-185.
60 Preston, 244.
61 Gullet, 724.
62 Great Britain, National Archives, Diary of General Headquarters Egyptian Expeditionary Force, 29 September 1918, WO 95/4371.

and sitting by fires. Sporadic rifle fire aimed at the Beni Sakr Arabs prompted cheers from the British: "Come on Jacko, give it to the blighters!"[63] Once the Arab threat dispersed, the Turks surrendered to the British in a state of near starvation, having had no water for hours, and with their uniforms in rags. They had remained loyal to their agreement with the British not only because of their condition and the threat posed by the enemy Arabs, but also because the British had treated them with dignity and respect. A key illustration of this treatment was the guarantee to Wahaby by Brigadier General G. de. L. Ryrie that no wounded Turks would be left behind.[64] The conclusion of this episode found Chaytor's Force having achieved all of its strategic goals. In the entire Jordan campaign, Chaytor's Force captured 10,300 men, 57 artillery pieces, 132 machine guns, eleven railroad engines and 106 trucks. In exchange, the force suffered three officers and 24 soldiers killed, ten officers and 95 soldiers wounded, and seven missing.[65] Chaytor and his men dealt a major blow to the Ottoman Fourth Army, which contributed to the decimation of that army in combination with subsequent attacks farther north conducted in part by the Arab allies of the British.

Chaytor's last operations were collectively one of three last British offensives in the Battle of Megiddo. While the episode at Kastal unfolded, the last large scale cavalry operations of the Egyptian Expeditionary Force completed the destruction of the Ottoman and German defense of Palestine. The first of these was the seizure of the port of Haifa, which was logistically important to any further British advance north since the port facilities could be used to resupply the Egyptian Expeditionary Force from the sea. The operation to seize the port proved one of the most costly to the Desert Mounted Corps. At first on 22 September Chauvel ordered the 12th Light Armored Car Battery and the 7th Light Car Patrol against Haifa rather than mounted units of the corps as intelligence reports indicated that the Turks had already evacuated the port. The soldiers of these units quickly found the reports false as they captured 69 Ottoman soldiers at a railway bridge eight miles southwest of the port. Subsequently on approaching Haifa both units came under concerted machine gun and artillery fire and were forced to withdraw to Megiddo. This failure led to the deployment of the 15th Cavalry Brigade of the 5th Cavalry Division to Haifa. The task of taking Haifa certainly was daunting given the terrain that led to the port, which was easily defensible. The port rests at the foot of Mount Carmel. This geographic feature is a long, narrow ridge well suited to emplacements that can command the southern approach to Haifa. The northern approach to the port was equally problematic owing to the Nahr el Muqatta River and its tributaries. This river system and the swampy land surrounding it was dangerous for horse and rider alike. On the approach of the 15th Cavalry Brigade to Haifa, quicksand around the Nahr el Muqatta claimed the lives of

63 Gullet, 727.
64 Australian War Memorial, Diary of the 2nd Australian Light Horse Brigade, 29 September 1918, AWM 4 10/2/45.
65 Gullet, 727.

two guides of the force.⁶⁶ The British then launched an assault on Mount Carmel that took the defenses on the ridge before attacking the port. This duty fell to the Jodhpore Lancers under the command of Colonel Dalpat Singh. The Lancers rode straight into the city under concerted machine gun fire to their front and flanks. Even so, by the end of the day Haifa lay in the hands of the British with the capture of 25 Ottoman officers, 664 soldiers, 16 artillery pieces, and then machine guns. These numbers as well as the capture cost three killed and 34 wounded of the Jodhpore Lancers. Among these was Colonel Singh whose ride into the city elicited specific praise from General Allenby on 24 September in a letter to Sir Pertab Singh:

> Congratulate you on the brilliant exploit of your regiment the Jodhpur Lancers, who on the twenty-third September took the town of Haifa at a gallop, killing many Turks with the lance in the streets of the town…Their gallant Colonel, Dalpat Singh, fell gloriously at the head of his regiment. He was buried with full military honors this afternoon.⁶⁷

The British also suffered 60 horses killed and an additional 83 wounded. Such losses proved acceptable in the mind of Allenby, however, due to Haifa's strategic importance. The British promptly installed a military governor in Haifa.⁶⁸ This proved the first step towards making the port a logistical center for further operations north.

While the taking of Haifa unfolded so too did efforts of the 4th Cavalry Division to capture more Turks retreating north. Chauvel received intelligence reports that the last retreating Turks involved in the Ottoman defense of Palestine were trying to cross the Jordan River at a point farther south than elements of the 4th Cavalry in order to escape capture. On 23 September Chauvel consequently ordered the 4th Cavalry Division's 11th Brigade to ride south down the river to bar the Turkish exit. The result was the sighting of a large column of Ottoman troops trying to cross the Jordan River at Makhadet Abu Naji. The riders of the brigade managed to take 800 prisoners including General Rushdi Bey, the commander of the Turkish 16th Division attached to the German Asia Korps.

The final cavalry operation proved the most crucial of the three. This was the assault on 25 September of the Australian Mounted Division against the Turkish defended town of Samakh on the southern tip of the Sea of Galilee. This town proved critical to General Liman von Sanders' efforts to reverse the disastrous strategic situation of his forces. By 25 September, both the Ottoman Seventh and the Eighth Armies were

---

66   Preston, 235.
67   For numbers of casualties for both the Ottomans and British at Haifa, see Preston, 537. For the letter of congratulations see Savage, Raymond. *Allenby of Armageddon: A Record of the Career and Campaigns of Field-Marshal Viscount Allenby* (Indianapolis, IN: Bobbs-Merrill, 1926), 301.
68   Great Britain, National Archives, "Moves and Organization", 22 September 1918, Diary of the General Headquarters Egyptian Expeditionary Force, WO 95/4371.

destroyed and all of Palestine west of the Jordan River was under the command of the British Egyptian Expeditionary Force. Sanders envisioned Samakh as part of a new defensive line that ran west from Deraa in the east along the Yarmuk River and through Samakh in the center of the new line. He hoped that this new position would allow for the defense of Damascus, Syria versus the British advance. Conversely, the British resolved to render any Ottoman attempt to do this moot through the conquest of Samakh.

Tasked with the assault was the 4th Light Horse Brigade of the Australian Mounted Corps under the command of Brigadier General Grant. The assault proved a fiercely contested one owing to two factors. First, was the well-established defense of Samakh by both German and Turkish troops along stone walls and within the buildings of the town. Secondly, Grant's forces encountered a growing problem for the British as they pushed farther north in operations that eventually took them out of Palestine into Syria: the diminution of their force strength due to garrisoning newly conquered regions and having to guard the masses of Ottoman and German prisoners of war. Even so, Grant ordered the 11th Australian Light Horse Brigade to make a mounted attack against the city with the 12th Australian Light Horse Brigade in reserve. Within one hour the British commanded Samakh, but at a high cost indicative of the strong Ottoman defense and denuded numbers of the British force. Some 100 Germans were killed while 364 Ottomans and Turks were taken as prisoners of war. The Australian casualties amounted to 78 killed and wounded with the additional loss of 100 horses.[69] Such Ottoman losses produced a situation where the defensive position of General Liman von Sanders lay in ruins.

The capture of Samakh ended the operation of the Battle of Megiddo. With the fall of the town the British achieved the strategic goals of General Edmund Allenby. Palestine, as well as the lands west of the Jordan River and north to Deraa, which remained Ottoman as of 25 September, now lay in British hands. The fall of Samakh, however, proved much more important than simply being the end of British operations during and as a result of the Battle of Megiddo. It resulted in the destruction of Ottoman attempts to re-establish a defense against the advance of the Egyptian Expeditionary Force. As such, Allenby had a strategic opportunity that lay beyond the objectives of his original plan. The Egyptian Expeditionary Force, thanks to the Battle of Megiddo, was poised for further operations north into Syria against primarily Damascus and still farther north to southern Turkey, the heart of the Ottoman Empire.

69 Perrett, 65.

5

Military and Political Ramifications

Advances by the Egyptian Expeditionary Force farther north than the Sea of Galilee were not part of the original operational plans for the Battle of Megiddo. General Allenby shared no such plans with his commanders in the series of briefings before the operation. Even so, the smashing success of the offensive led to Allenby envisioning additional offensives into the heart of Syria as Megiddo unfolded. Having expected heavy fighting in the regions of Jenin and Beisan, he was surprised at the total collapse of Ottoman defenses. A 22 September meeting at Megiddo between Allenby and Lieutenant General Chauvel was the origin of Allenby's strategic plan to push farther north by capitalizing on the Egyptian Expeditionary Force's recent success. His aim was to cause further damage to the Ottoman Army. At that meeting Allenby asked Chauvel to give numbers for the prisoners of war taken by the 5th Cavalry Division. When Chauvel reported 15,000 prisoners of war it elicited a laugh from Allenby as he exclaimed 'No bloody good to me! I want 30,000 before you're done!'[1] More telling as to the general's ambition was an abrupt comment made to Chauvel at the same meeting. When Chauvel reported that scarcely a Turk had gotten past the Desert Mounted Corps in the Plain of Esdraelon Allenby abruptly commented 'What about Damascus?'[2] Not only was Allenby envisioning a further assault north at the expense of the Turks, but so was the British government as Prime Minister Lloyd George's administration envisioned attacks as far as Aleppo. Allenby, given his conviction, and in response to the government's call for further action, laid out his plan in a 23 September letter to Field Marshal Sir Henry Wilson, Chief of the Imperial General Staff: "I have your…wire … proposing a Cavalry raid to Aleppo. I don't think Aleppo possible; but am sending 3 Divisions of Cavalry, as

---

1   Alec Hill, *Chauvel of the Light Horse: A Biography of General Sir Harry Chauvel* (Melbourne, Australia: Melbourne University Press, 1978), 172.
2   H.S. Gullet, *The Official History of Australia in the War of 1914-1918*, Vol. 7, *Sinai and Palestine: The Australian Imperial Force in Sinai and Palestine, 1914-1918* (Sydney: Angus and Robertson, 1923), 728.

soon as I can, to Damascus."³ The general's reservations concerning Aleppo stemmed from concerns over logistical support so far north and the general fatigue of his forces that could especially decrease the cavalry's combat efficiency. With his new objective of Damascus in mind, Allenby held a conference on 24 September at Jenin with Lieutenant Generals Chauvel, Chetwode, and Bulfin where he outlined his plan to take Damascus. While he did not believe that there would be serious opposition at Damascus, Allenby was concerned that the situation could change if the Ottoman Fourth Army, at the time retreating north to Deraa, got to the city ahead of Chauvel's forces. In order to avoid this situation Allenby issued orders for the 4th Cavalry Division to ride to Deraa from Beisan in the hopes of linking up with Emir Feisal's Arab Army and possibly destroying the Fourth Army. From there, the two forces would march north on the pilgrim road to Damascus. At the same time the 5th Cavalry Division and the Australian Mounted Division would ride north on the direct route to Damscus.⁴ Allenby desired all forces to arrive simultaneously at Damascus for the offensive to take the city.

The operations of the 4th Cavalry Division were greatly supported by the Arab Army, which proved crucial in seizing the town of Deraa. The cavalry division's advance halted due to stiffening Turkish resistance by the Ottoman Fourth Army that held defensive positions at the villages of El Bahira and Irbid to the east of Beisan. Whilst El Bahira was secured on 26 September, the Ottoman defense in Irbid repelled an attack by the 2nd Lancers before withdrawing during the night. Only in the morning did the advance of the 4th Cavalry Division continue until Major General Barrow halted the division a few miles outside of Deraa. Not only were his horses tired from the advance and riding down Turks retreating towards the town, but he was also unsure as to who held Deraa. Ascertaining the status of the town proved wise. Barrow learned on 28 September from Colonel T.E. Lawrence, the British liaison attached to the Arab Army, that the Arab Army had taken the town the previous afternoon following concerted British bombing attacks in the days prior. What Barrow found in Deraa when he rode into the town that morning was a testimony to the disastrous and desperate situation of General Djemal Kucek's retreating Ottoman Fourth Army: "the whole place was indescribably filthy, defiled, and littered … Turks, some dead and some dying, lay about the railway station or sat propped up against houses."⁵ The state of affairs in Deraa was also a matter of great contention between himself, Lawrence, and the Arab Army as a whole. Barrow encountered an ambulance train at the station full of wounded and sick Turkish soldiers. Here he observed "Arab soldiers…going through the train, tearing off the clothing of the

---

3   Allenby to Wilson, 23 September 1918, in Matthew Hughes, ed., *Allenby in Palestine: The Middle East Correspondence of Field Marshal Viscount Allenby, June 1917-October 1919* (Stroud: Sutton Publishing, 2004), 183.
4   Great Britain, National Archives, Diary of the General Staff of the Desert Mounted Corps, 26 September 1918, WO 95/4473.
5   George de S Barrow, *The Fire of Life* (London: Hutchinson, 1942), 211.

groaning and stricken Turks, regardless of gaping wounds and broken limbs, and cutting their victims' throats."[6] Barrow promptly removed the Arabs from the train upon Lawrence's refusal to do so as he stated it was their idea of war. Barrow's disgust over the incident and with Lawrence continued in the years following the conclusion of the war. The dead, dying, and looted Turks of Deraa, however, represented only a small portion of the Ottoman Fourth Army. General Kucek's force remained largely intact as he succeeded in withdrawing the bulk of his force towards Damascus before the town fell. The only exception was the II Corps, being the unit captured by the British during the retreat to Deraa.

From Deraa both the 4th Cavalry Division and the Arab Army rode in pursuit of the Ottoman Fourth Army while the other units earmarked for the assault on Damascus, being the 5th Cavalry Division and Australian Mounted Division, had begun their march on 27 September. The advance proved fraught with problems particularly for the latter two divisions. One difficulty lay in the advance being slowed by Turkish demolition of bridges and roads that led to Damascus, an example being the bridge at Jisr Benat Yakub that lay at the site of the farthest advance of Napoleon with his Army of Egypt during the French Revolutionary Wars. While these could be repaired fairly quickly a further problem lay with a general lack of British intelligence on the terrain over which the cavalry had to pass to get to Damascus. Damascus lay so far north of the position of the Egyptian Expeditionary Force at the opening of the Battle of Megiddo that the fine aerial reconnaissance garnered by Allied aircraft previous to the operation was no longer of any use. What maps the British forces did have were inaccurate and lacking in detail. One key detail missing from the maps was the steep and rocky hills that lay all the way to the western approach of Damascus that was almost impassable to cavalry. The path known as the Beirut Road was quite difficult as it ran at the bottom of Barada Gorge into which the cavalry could not descend. The other path was the Homs Road on which the Australian Mounted Division encountered some resistance on 29 September at Sa'sa before continuing to advance north while riding down retreating Turks and Germans.

By 29 September all British units involved in the advance on Damascus steadily closed in on the town while engaging elements of the retreating Ottoman Fourth Army as it attempted to reach Damascus. As the 4th Cavalry and Arab Army pursued General Djemal Kucek's army as it retreated through Barada Gorge, elements of the Australian Mounted Division occupied the heights over the gorge on 30 September in order to ambush the retreating Turks. This proved devastating as the gorge itself is only 100 yards wide and thus allowed for no maneuver for the Ottomans and Germans that were with them as the Australians poured concerted fire into the gorge. The result was a grim spectacle where for miles 400 dead Ottoman and German soldiers littered the ground amidst destroyed equipment.[7] Throughout that night the

---

6   Barrow, 211.
7   Bryan Perrett, *Megiddo 1918: Lawrence, Allenby, and the March on Damascus* (Westport, Conn.: Praeger, 2004), 78.

remaining broken columns of Fourth Army continued their retreat bound for Homs and Aleppo as General Djemal Kucek deemed Damascus as indefensible. Part of that belief rested in the fact that a large portion of the city's population were Arab and Christian and thus possibly more sympathetic to the Allies than the Ottomans. Indeed, this estimation proved to be the case. The city's military governor, Ali Riza Pasha, was an individual educated at the Turkish Military Academy and a serving officer of the Ottoman Army. Even so, he was also an Arab. As British forces closed in on Damascus, Ali Riza Pasha despite his orders to hold Damascus rode out of the city and presented Lieutenant General Barrow with the defensive plans designed to hold it. The result was that the British rode into Damascus virtually unopposed with the Australian Mounted Division first entering the city on 1 October.

The conquest of Damascus, despite the obvious military triumph for the Egyptian Expeditionary Force, actually presented strategic problems as well as political ones. The seizure of Damascus certainly had negative consequences for the fighting condition of Chauvel's Desert Mounted Corps. The immediate problem was the maintenance of order in the city. Damascus at the time had a population of some 300,000 people and, while the Australians rode into the city amidst great celebration, violence erupted throughout the morning of 1 October and into the morning of 2 October. Only a triumphal march of British cavalry through the city quelled the instability in a situation where Chauvel had to deal with using his cavalry to garrison Damascus rather than mount further operations against the Turks. In addition, the drive to Damascus and the capture of the city required the British to take care of some 20,000 prisoners of war.[8] Finally and perhaps the greatest detriment to the condition of the Desert Mounted Corps upon the capture of Damascus was the problem of disease. The condition of the city made it a breeding ground for diseases because the retreating Turks left behind hospitals full of dead or dying Turks with few supplies to aid them.

This situation only compounded a problem that was a mounting one for the Desert Mounted Corps throughout the Battle of Megiddo. Over the period between 19 September and 30 September the three cavalry divisions of the Desert Mounted Corps had ridden 200 miles, captured more than 60,000 prisoners, 140 artillery pieces, and 500 machine guns while existing on half rations.[9] Men and horse alike were tired and undernourished on reaching Damascus. In addition, the riders of the corps had passed through territory that was disease ridden and thus had fallen victim to illness. The majority of those inflicted were cases of malaria from areas around the Jordan River and Beisan. In the case of the latter, the British had discarded their mosquito nets in order to move more quickly.[10] Making matters still worse was the

---

8   Archibald Wavell, *Allenby: A Study in Greatness* (New York: Oxford University Press, 1941), 230.
9   R.M.P. Preston, *The Desert Mounted Corps: An Account of the Cavalry Operations in Palestine and Syria, 1917-1918* (New York: Houghton Mifflin, 1923), 283.
10 Great Britain, National Archives, Diary of the 11th Cavalry Brigade, Desert Mounted Corps. A History of Operations, WO 95/4510.

fact that the drive to Damascus had resulted in the Desert Mounted Corps advancing beyond their logistical net to include their medical staff, which meant that there was no quinine to combat the malaria. The result was the death of many British soldiers and the incapacitation of others. The Desert Mounted Corps' R.H. Wilson recounted the state of himself and his comrades in Damascus as they suffered with the illness:

> There were about twenty of us in the room where I was put, and not a soul came to see us until the third night. My Squadron Sgt. Major was lying dead in the doorway, and anyone who was fit enough to go for water had to step or crawl over him. A Corporal in my troop was dead in the passage just outside ... A Subaltern in my Regiment, a good friend of mine, spent practically the whole of the time, day and night, shrieking at the top of his voice, and jumping up from his stretcher, until he finally collapsed. For the two days and three nights I did not move, but the ague caused me to shake to such an extent that my stretcher had travelled nearly half way across the room.[11]

In this situation, only the 5th Cavalry Division was in marginally good condition. Even so, cases of malaria were present in the division in addition to influenza that afflicted ultimately all three divisions of the Desert Mounted Corps.

Another of Allenby's problems was the political ramifications of the conquest of Damascus. This was the first time that political questions concerning the future of the Middle East came into play as a direct result of the British conquest of Turkish territory. With its mostly Arab population, Damascus was claimed as the focal point of the pan-Arab state promised by the British in return for Arab participation in the war as part of the Allied cause. A reflection of this commitment was in the orders issued by Allenby that Emir Feisal should hoist the Sheriffian flag of the Arabs over Damascus as his forced entered the city.[12] Even so, hoisting the flag in the minds of Allenby, the British as whole, or the French did not mean that the city was under Arab control. For the latter, Damascus lay in the zone of French influence according to the Sykes-Picot Agreement. The conflicting claims of the French and the Arabs consequently led Allenby to table any political considerations while the war was still in progress in the name of not compromising the war effort against the Ottomans. Allenby had the backing of Chief of the Imperial General Staff Wilson who on 25 August had told Allenby that whatever was to be decided in the region politically would be subject to Allenby's authority and that military considerations took precedence over political ones.[13] As a result Allenby ordered Chauvel to administer Damascus in a manner similar to that employed with the conquest of Jerusalem. Chauvel had orders to retain

---

11 Great Britain, Imperial War Museum, Wilson R.H. MSS 72/25/1, 66.
12 Great Britain, National Archives, Minutes of the War Cabinet, 2 October 1918, CAB 23/8, 2.
13 Lawrence James, *Imperial Warrior: The Life and Times of Field-Marshal Viscount Allenby, 1861-1936* (London: Weidenfeld and Nicolson, 1993), 168.

the existing local governor and administrative structures while making them answerable to the British.

The problem with this course lay with Emir Feisal who was not willing to compromise his goal of a pan-Arab state. Indeed, unbeknownst to Allenby, Lawrence had already counseled Feisal to claim the city by right of conquest as soon as possible. Feisal's attempt to do so centered on the question of which Allied forces had ridden into Damascus first. Feisal claimed that the Arabs had arrived ahead of British forces and thus had a claim to Damascus as a prize of war. While it was clearly the forces of the Australian Mounted Division that arrived first, the problem of control still remained. Lawrence, who was sympathetic to the Arab cause, had staged a coup in Damascus during the morning of 1 October before the Arab Army's arrival that placed Shukri el Ayubi, who was pro-Feisal, in the position of governor. At first, Chauvel on his arrival to Damascus accepted Shukri on the grounds that the majority of Arabs in Damascus supported him. His stance, however, changed when he realized the role of Lawrence and his goals for Feisal. At that point, Chauvel removed Shukri in keeping with the spirit of his orders from Allenby and replaced him with Ali Riza Rikabi. The new governor was an Arab nationalist, but also a former officer of the Ottoman Army. These events, in addition to general lawlessness in the city, accounted for the reason why Chauvel ordered the 2 October triumphal march of British cavalry through Damascus to emphasize that Damascus lay in the hands of the British. Even the installment of Rikabi and this march, however, did not end the situation between the British and Arabs as Lawrence planned a triumphal march for Feisal on 3 October as response to that of Chauvel. The situation in Damascus was the first of many in the context of the overlapping agreements signed by the Allied powers for the Middle East after the war. The Battle of Megiddo made possible the potential implementation of these agreements with all of the problems associated with them.

General Allenby was fully aware of the instability that disagreements such as those in Damascus could cause. Being devoted solely to matters of military efficiency at the time rather than political questions, the issue of control in Damascus prompted Allenby to visit the city where he met Emir Feisal at the Hotel Victoria. The afternoon meeting there, while designed to foster a degree of stability, also laid bare the political problems of the Middle East. Allenby asserted military control of Damascus but also explained to Feisal that the French would be the future protecting power of not only Damascus, but all of Syria in keeping with the Sykes-Picot Agreement. Within this arrangement Feisal representing his father King Hussein would administer governance in Syria with French financial assistance and political guidance. Allenby also told Feisal that only the hinterland of Syria would be under the direct control of a future pan-Arab state and specifically stated that Lebanon lay outside the Arab jurisdiction.[14] The clearly overlapping and muddled nature of Allenby's directives were a reflection of

---

14 Copy of Record written by Lt. Gen. Sir H.G. Chauvel. Meeting of Sir Edmund Allenby and the Emir Feisal at the Hotel Victoria, Damascus, on Oct. 3rd, 1918, 22 October

the state of affairs for the British government as they faced diplomatic pressure from both their French and Arab allies. Feisal's reaction was one of surprise and strenuous objection, but he was forced to yield to Allenby as the general reminded him that he was a lieutenant general under his command and must thereby obey his orders.

The settling of matters over Damascus still did not put an end to the political questions that dogged the final stages of the British military effort in the near Middle East. Indeed, problems elsewhere over the same conflicting diplomatic agreements convinced Allenby that he faced a serious and intractable problem. On the same day as Allenby's meeting with Feisal, a pro-Feisal coup occurred in the port city of Beirut. The city, having been evacuated by retreating Ottoman forces, was one that Allenby had earmarked as a forward supply base for his forces in northern Syria. Matters became serious on 6 October when a French destroyer escorting transports arrived in the harbor to unload supplies and claim the city as part of France's territory granted by the Sykes-Picot Agreement. While the presence of the French naval units sparked great tension, so too did the installation of French Colonel P. de Piepape as military governor. Piepape was the commander of the Detachement Francais de Palestine et Syrie, which was the small contingent of French under the command of Allenby. Piepape as governor began to congratulate those in Beirut and Syria for coming under the political control of France. This prompted Allenby to remind the colonel that "he has nothing to do with politics; and that he is an officer of mine, responsible to me for the Civil Administration of Occupied Enemy Territory North of Palestine."[15] The situation in Beirut as well as Damascus led Allenby to identify rising Franco-phobia in Syria and Lebanon as a threat to his military authority. In an effort to stave off any additional problems, Allenby on 23 October issued new orders for overseeing captured enemy territory. These orders called for the British to militarily administer Palestine while the French did the same in a coastal strip of land from Beirut to Alexandretta. A third region from Aquaba to Aleppo was placed under Ali Riza Rikabi, the military governor of Damscus.[16] While Allenby struggled mightily to maintain the territory captured by the Battle of Megiddo and its aftermath, political events severely challenged his efforts.

Whilst these events burdened Allenby in his pursuit of governing the territory seized by his command, the general had already decided to increase the area of the captured land under his control. Allenby had ordered a further advance north from Damascus to Aleppo. While he had strenuously resisted this course of action when broached by Chief of the Imperial General Staff Wilson owing to lack of force strength, Allenby came to believe that it was an acceptable risk to strike a political blow against the Ottomans with an advance to southern Turkey. The operation was

1929, in Matthew Hughes, ed., *Allenby in Palestine: The Middle East Correspondence of Field Marshal Viscount Allenby, June 1917-October 1919*, 297-298.
15 Allenby to Wilson, 19 October 1918, in Matthew Hughes, ed., *Allenby in Palestine: The Middle East Correspondence of Field Marshal Viscount Allenby, June 1917-October 1919*, 208.
16 James, 173.

certainly a calculated risk given the condition of the Desert Mounted Corps. Due to the outbreak of malaria and influenza combined with the strain of prolonged operations neither the 4th Cavalry Division nor the Australian Mounted Division were able to mount further operations. This left only Major General Macandrew's 5th Cavalry Division and it was also in a much reduced state. Upon receiving orders to advance north Macandrew had only 1,500 cavalrymen under his command. At the same time, British intelligence believed that some 20,000 Germans and Ottomans lay at or around Aleppo.[17] Allenby consequently ordered that the 2nd, 11th, and 12th Light Armoured Motor Batteries and the 1st, 2nd, and 7th Light Car Patrols be attached to Macandrew's command.

The advance to Aleppo proved relatively easy given that there was little fighting owing to the Ottomans being in retreat north. The major railroad junction of Riyaq fell on 6 October after being abandoned by the Turks. The port of Tripoli fell in a similar fashion on 26 October thus giving Allenby another port for logistical support of his force. The assault proved only slightly more difficult as the Turkish defenders of Aleppo, under the command of General Mustapha Kemal, were already preparing a retreat farther north. Arab forces entered the city on the night 25 October and after a short but sharp encounter with Turkish soldiers took Aleppo. Macandrew entered Aleppo the following day as Kemal's forces occupied defensive positions 20 miles north of Aleppo in the hills on the Alexandretta Road. The capture of Aleppo proved to be the last offensive of the Egyptian Expeditionary Force. Whilst Allenby's army, due to the condition of the Desert Mounted Corps, was incapable of further sustained operations, the British were able to not only achieve all of the objectives of their original offensive, but also much more owing to Allenby's success.

This achievement came at relatively little cost in relation to so many of the great operations of the war. Indeed, the Battle of Megiddo and the subsequent offensives constituted some of the greatest Allied successes of the war in terms of the number of soldiers lost in comparison to that of the enemy including prisoners of war. By late October 1918 the Ottoman Army had suffered the loss of all of Palestine and Syria with the destruction of the Seventh and Eighth armies and the decimation of the Ottoman Fourth Army. The degree of devastation was such that official figures for the combat losses of the Ottomans between 19 September and the end of October 1918 are unknown. This is attributable to the destruction of the army headquarters of both the Ottoman Seventh and Eighth armies.[18] What is more precisely known are the number of soldiers and the amount of equipment captured form the Yildirim Army Group owing to British records. The total number of prisoners exceeded 75,000 with 200 of these being officers and 3,500 being Germans and a few Austrians. The British also seized 360 artillery pieces, 800 machine guns, 210 trucks, 89 railroad

17   Preston, 287.
18   Edward Erickson, *Ordered to Die: A History of the Ottoman Army in the First World War* (London: Greenwood Press, 2001), 201.

locomotives, and 468 railroad cars. The destruction of the Ottoman armies came at a cost among the officer corps of 71 killed, 249 wounded, and three missing in action. The regular ranks suffered 782 killed, 4,179 wounded, and 382 missing in action. All told the British lost only 5,666 men with the losses of the Desert Mounted Corps, being the spearhead of the operations, amounting to 650 dead.[19]

The combat losses of the Ottomans as well as the territorial loss of Palestine and Syria, however, did not convince the Ottoman government to withdraw from the war. Rather, the advance of Allied forces from conquered Bulgaria towards Thrace and Istanbul was the immediate cause. Even so, Megiddo is tangentially responsible for the Ottoman exit from the war as the force strength in Thrace was not adequate owing to the siphoning of troops to other fronts including Palestine and Syria. In addition, the loss of so many soldiers in Palestine and Syria as a result of the Battle of Megiddo meant that there was no way to augment Ottoman forces in Thrace. The dire situation forced the Ottomans to sign an armistice on 30 October 1918 at Mudros.[20] Indeed, they had little choice. Losses in Palestine and Syria certainly produced a situation whereby the Ottomans lacked the resources to reverse their declining fortunes. Edward Erickson likens the Battle of Megiddo and subsequent operations to Ludendorff's "Black Day" of 8 August 1918 in terms of the catastrophe. Indeed, the Ottoman strategic focus by late October 1918 rested solely on retaining as much territory as possible rather than reversing their fortunes on the battlefield.[21] To this end, Megiddo precipitated a change in leadership on 30 October 1918 with the removal of Enver Pasha as Minister of War in favor of Ahmet Izzet Pasha. In addition, General Mustapha Kemal replaced General Liman von Sanders as the commander of the remnants of Yildirim Army Group. The mission of Yildirim Army Group became the protection of the Anatolian heartland should the armistice not hold.

By the time that Mustapha Kemal assumed command he was already well aware that his forces were largely incapable of mounting further operations thanks to the Battle of Megiddo, nor participating in the operations that unfolded subsequent to it. During the Arab occupation of Damascus, Kemal had a staff meeting at Rayak, the newly established headquarters for the German Asia Korps, to discuss the creation of new defensive positions against the British. His exchange with a German colonel offers a stark illustration of the Ottoman position. Kemal asked the colonel for the disposition of German and Turkish troops still under his command as well as their strength. The colonel replied that he could provide no intelligence on the disposition of troops and went so far as to say that he had no cohesive force. This prompted Kemal to remark, "Which means I have before me a colonel with his staff and nothing else?"

---

19 For all figures see Cyril Falls, *History of the Great War, based on Official Documents, Military Operations Egypt and Palestine, 1914-1918*. Volume II. *From June 1917 to the End of the War* (London: HMSO, 1930), 618.
20 Erickson, *Ordered to Die*, 204.
21 Erickson, *Ordered to Die*, 204.

to which the colonel replied, "That is so."²² Ultimately, Kemal was able to assemble two divisions of Ottoman and German troops. They represented the extent of Ottoman power in the wake of Megiddo. The two divisions faced the potential of being overrun should the Egyptian Expeditionary Force manage to concentrate its forces. By the time of the armistice, Kemal's two divisions occupied the heights north of the Aleppo.

The condition of Kemal's forces as well as their geographic position was the result of one of the most successful offensives of the First World War. In the space of six weeks, Allenby's Egyptian Expeditionary Force had advanced 350 miles. Allenby, hailed as a hero at the end of the war, had already given the credit to his troops in a 26 September 1918 message:

> I desire to convey to all ranks and all arms of the Force under my command, my admiration and thanks for their great deeds ... and my appreciation of their gallantry and determination, which have resulted in the destruction of the VIIth and VIIIth Turkish Armies opposed to us. Such a complete victory has seldom been known in all the history of war.²³

The entire campaign was a tribute to thorough preparation, deception of the enemy, and a concentration of force strength in order to smash through enemy positions.

Whilst the Battle of Megiddo was indeed one of the most decisive offensives of 1914-18, the battle plan that produced the success can hardly be considered revolutionary. Allenby was not a great visionary strategically. Indeed, some of Allenby's contemporaries viewed the outcome of the Battle of Megiddo as having little to do with Allenby himself. Secretary to the War Cabinet Maurice Hankey wrote on 23 September in his diary that "the Palestine victory is largely due to...refusing to allow the transport of the 54th Division from Palestine to the Western Front. As C.I.G.S. said to me this afternoon, the victories in Palestine and Salonika are most glaring examples of "amateur strategy" – but he is very pleased all the same.²⁴ Comments such as these are certainly faint praise.

Despite the unoriginal nature of the plan, Allenby does deserve credit as one of the most successful generals of the First World War. Rather than being a visionary, Allenby's shining achievement was the wedding of new technology such as the airplane and armored car to a strategy that had at its core one of the oldest arms of the military, the cavalry, into combined arms operations. In addition, Allenby's great success comes from his being a de-centralizer in terms of leadership. Once the operational

---

22 Kinross, Lord, *Ataturk: A Biography of Mustapha Kemal, Father of Modern Turkey* (New York: William Morrow and Company, 1965), 142.
23 Allenby to his Command, 26 September 1918, in Matthew Hughes, ed., *Allenby in Palestine: The Middle East Correspondence of Field Marshal Viscount Allenby, June 1917-October 1919*, 189.
24 Maurice Hankey, *The Supreme Command, 1914-1918* (London: George Allen and Unwin, 1961), 839.

orders for the Battle of Megiddo were in place, Allenby trusted his corps commanders and junior officers to execute them in the spirit that they were given. Finally, Allenby owed much of his success to the training of the Egyptian Expeditionary Force by his junior officers when he himself doubted the fighting ability of his force in the wake of its reorganization. A crucial element amongst those newly trained troops were the Indians who contributed mightily to the outcome of the Battle of Megiddo.

The smashing military success against the Ottomans, however, was not one that Allenby could savor in the immediate aftermath of the armistice with the Turks. The reason was that Allenby had to quickly focus his labors once again on the political questions arising from the success enjoyed in the Battle of Megiddo and the subsequent campaigns. Indeed, the general had already been transitioning to a political role with the events surrounding control of Damascus and with the French in Haifa that were a reflection of the agreements signed that would determine the political map of the Middle East. The British looked very quickly to the post-war world in the Middle East where Allenby assumed a central role. This began even before the armistice as London advised the Turks that they discuss with Allenby the terms of the armistice. It is certainly not surprising that London chose Allenby to lead the discussions concerning the armistice. He was the sole authority in a geographic area where he commanded the only Allied army, the Egyptian Expeditionary Force, in a region that stretched from Cilicia in the north to the Sinai in the south and from the Mediterranean Sea to the deserts east of the Jordan River. This area encompassed all of modern-day Palestine, Syria, and Lebanon and held some one million people.[25] Within this area there was a virtual political vacuum with the end of Ottoman rule.

Allenby was already well aware of the instability posed by this situation and had taken some steps prior to the armistice to deal with it. His policy rested on his treating all captured territory from the standpoint of being a military governor. His initial problem after the conclusion of hostilities proved to be the Turks themselves. North of Aleppo some Turkish soldiers chose to disregard the armistice, which induced the Turkish government to begin to try and negotiate the terms of the armistice already in place. Allenby's response was prompt as he boarded a French warship and went to Istanbul for a personal meeting with the Turkish Minister of Foreign Affairs as well as the Minister of War. Allenby later detailed that he "gravely told them why I had come, and, refusing to hear any arguments, I left them the text of my demands in English and in Turkish. They were taken quite aback; and I do not think they will forget it while they live."[26] The exchange promptly brought an end to the actions of the Turkish soldiers north of Aleppo as well as the efforts of the Turkish government to alter the terms of the armistice.

---

25 James, 179.
26 Brian Gardner, *Allenby of Arabia: Lawrence's General* (New York: Coward-McCann, 1965), 214.

Dealing with the Turks proved the least of Allenby's challenges as he quickly had to address again mounting problems from the political agreements signed over the course of the war for the post-war Middle East. Allenby was not well equipped to handle this task past treating the region as a military governor. Indeed, on 7 November 1917 when he arrived in the theater it was obvious that Allenby was unaware of the post-war designs of the Allied powers and Arabs. Allenby pledged that the only goal of the Allied powers in the Middle East was to establish governments based on the self-determination of Arab peoples. By late 1918, Allenby realized the folly of that pledge as he knew well by that time the nature of the diplomatic agreements and viewed them as wholly unworkable for the region since they were all conflicting in nature. In this light he continued to spearhead his efforts to maintain stability in the region through the creation on 19 October 1918 of the Occupied Enemy Territory Administration. Within this administrative machinery Allenby carved up British held territory into two regions. The first was Occupied Enemy Territory South under the command of General Money that included the regions around Jerusalem, Nablus, and Acre. The second, known as Occupied Enemy Territory East which was under Ali Riza Pasha el Rikabi aegis and extended to all districts east of the prior territory as well as those north. Both of these sectors were governed under the administration of military law and Allenby forbade any departure from that law in an effort to quell any political problems that might destabilize the region.[27] A reflection of Allenby's concern in this regard is evident in a 29 October 1918 telegram to the War Office that those areas east of the Jordan in the region of Es Salt and Amman, being coveted by the Arabs, would only be under tenuous control of a British officer safeguarding the inhabitants of the areas until the Arabs could establish an administration. Additionally, the city of Damascus, already occupied by Arabs, was to remain under their control. Finally, all areas intended by the French as part of their dominion in Syria by the terms of the Sykes-Picot agreement would be under the control of French officials answerable to Allenby.[28]

The latter terms with the French clearly denoted the tortured nature of the political environment in the Middle East after the war with multiple agents having territorial goals in the region. As Allenby put the machinery of the Occupied Enemy Territory Administration in place the British government knew that the situation was a poor one particularly in regard to the Sykes-Picot Agreement that threatened diplomatic clashes with Britain and its French and Arab Allies. On 29 October 1918 in a meeting of the War Cabinet Lord Curzon commented that "Syria was likely to be the scene of great anxiety to us in the future. We had conquered the country, and the French wanted the spoils. This would necessarily bring us in as third parties to any dispute

27 Allenby to War Office, 23 October 1918, in Matthew Hughes, ed., *Allenby in Palestine: The Middle East Correspondence of Field Marshal Viscount Allenby, June 1917-October 1919*, 211.
28 Great Britain, National Archives, Political Intelligence Diary, 29 October 1918, WO 157/731.

between the French and the Arabs.[29] Indeed, this fear was quickly realized at the opening of November as the French in Beirut began releasing propaganda heralding the coming of the French protectorate in their zone of influence under the Sykes-Picot Agreement. This was not sanctioned by Allenby and was viewed by Emir Feisal as a threat to his Arab cause.

In this atmosphere London looked to scrapping the Sykes-Picot Agreement that threatened the stability of the region. On 7 November 1918 Lloyd George's government issued a declaration for the Middle East based on United States President Woodrow Wilson's call for the self-determination of peoples. This declaration called for the construction of national governments and administrations whose authority came from the indigenous populations of the region.[30] The reasons for the shift to this stance rested on the desire of the British to limit French power in the Middle East while furthering their own. David Lloyd George's government desired a revision of the original British territory envisioned in the Sykes-Picot Agreement as under British control and including suzerainty over the oil rich city of Mosul and direct control over Palestine. This goal that lay at the heart of the new declaration was not a new one. By late 1918 there was much opposition in London to the Sykes-Picot Agreement because it limited British actions in the Middle East. The new declaration was the culmination of several meetings in 1918 of the Eastern Committee formed by Lloyd George to examine the course for revision of Sykes-Picot. Indeed, the Eastern Committee members envisioned a Middle East dominated by the British in order to have complete mastery of the territory that led east to India.[31] The path to accomplish this goal was to support Britain's Arab allies through the original 1916 agreement with them that had promised Arab self-determination and ran counter to the goals of the French. The central portion of this drive was the establishment of Emir Feisal as head of a government in Syria. The British saw this step as crucial to their interests. While supporting Woodrow Wilson's call for self-determination on the surface, the installation of Feisal would in reality produce a government sympathetic to British imperial interests in the Middle East. The Arabs were whole-heartedly opposed to French influence in Syria and viewed the British as the guarantors of their autonomous position in the post-war world. As a result, London believed they could manipulate the Arabs to their own ends. The French naturally bitterly opposed the new British stance but could merely protest it and try and maintain the spirit of the Sykes-Picot Agreement in a Middle East where they had few material means to resist the shift pursued by London.

---

29 Great Britain, National Archives, Minutes of the War Cabinet, 29 October 1918, CAB 23/8, 3.
30 Great Britain, National Archives, Foreign Office, "Draft of the Anglo-French Declaration, 18 August 1918, FO 371/3381, F 146.
31 Great Britain, National Archives, "Report of the Eastern Committee", June 1918, CAB 23/43.

The diplomatic shift of the Lloyd George Coalition government did little to improve Allenby's position as military governor of the Near Middle East. At the same time as the issuance of the new declaration in London, both Mark Sykes and Georges Picot, being the authors of the original agreement, were in the region and touring Beirut, Damascus, and Aleppo to gauge local opinion over the political questions that dogged the post-war Near Middle East. The visit led Sykes to believe that any attempt by the French to place their officials into power in Syria would result in serious instability. Indeed, while Allenby enjoyed the tacit support of Feisal for his efforts to govern occupied territory, he knew that this support was tenuous. This prompted Allenby to assure Feisal that the new League of Nations, through international law, would settle the problem of the Near Middle East in the best interests of the Arabs. Feisal in response threatened war in the case of any other outcome.[32] That threat greatly concerned Allenby as any such war would pit his Egyptian Expeditionary Force against his ally to keep order. It could also possibly destabilize the entire region to include British Egypt and Palestine with the latter being a British imperial interest.

This situation prompted Emir Feisal to make his case for an Arab state in the Middle East on 6 February 1919 at the Quai d'Orsay as part the Paris Peace Conference where an acrimonious atmosphere existed between British representatives and those of the Arabs and French. The same day that Feisal spoke at Quai d'Orsay, Georges Picot issued a protest in Paris accusing the British of obstructing French efforts to establish themselves in Syria. Indeed, Picot went so far as accusing that General Bulfin received horses from Emir Feisal and gave them as gifts only to those that supported the British and none to those that sided with the French in Syria.[33] Picot in his animosity to the British was certainly not alone as French Premier Georges Clemenceau shared the sentiment. Colonial Secretary Lord Milner consequently met with Clemenceau in early March and asserted that the British had no desire to force the French out of Syria, but the Arabs of Syria and Lebanon were clearly against French influence in the Near Middle East.[34] While this was disingenuous the assertion ran counter to the conclusions of the Eastern Committee. It reveals the efforts of British officials to deflect French suspicions that Britain sought to undermine Sykes-Picot for its own end.

Part of the British attempt to bolster their case against the French in Syria was an invitation issued on 12 March 1919 to Allenby to attend the peace conference. Allenby arrived in Paris on 19 March and, while not being a political creature, he stood opposed to French intentions in Syria. In his mind this was completely for the sake of stability in the region rather than to support British imperial goals for the Near Middle East. David Lloyd George, however, clearly saw Allenby as an asset to further

32 James, 182.
33 Great Britain, National Archives, War Office Correspondence, 11 February 1919, WO 32/5602.
34 David Lloyd George, *Memoirs of the Paris Peace Conference*, Volume II (New Haven, Conn.: Yale University Press, 1939), 678.

Britain's goals as on the day of his arrival he had lunch with the prime minister. At the lunch Lloyd George urged Allenby to give the French his view of Syria and that the French would not be tolerated there.[35] Allenby did just that at a 20 March 1919 meeting in which the French presented their case for dominance of Syria. When asked what he thought of the French occupation of Syria, Allenby replied that it would be resisted by all Muslims and especially the Arabs.[36] Allenby's comments did little to alter the diplomatic impasse, but it did lead to support by American, British, and French representatives at the peace conference for the establishment of a commission to ascertain the feelings of the Arabs in Syria over the question. This course, championed by President Woodrow Wilson, gained the tacit support of Clemenceau. The fact that the problem remained unresolved meant that the political future of the territory gained by the British in the Near Middle East from the Battle of Megiddo remained in question.

This situation extended to not only Syria, but also Palestine. Indeed, the question of Palestine's future was of far greater importance to the British than that of Syria. While Palestine through the Sykes-Picot agreement was originally intended to be an internationally administered area, Haifa and Acre would be British enclaves. Haifa was particularly important to British imperial designs in the Middle East as the intention was to link Haifa by railroad to Baghdad as under the Sykes-Picot Agreement Britain would have control of Mesopotamia with its oil fields. Establishing this link would allow for British control of territory that ran from the Mediterranean to India.[37] That stance, however, changed over the course of the war. Sykes on 7 April 1917 in a letter to Maurice Hankey intoned that British occupation of Palestine after the war was a *fait accompli* given its occupation by troops of the Egyptian Expeditionary Force.[38] By October 1918, the British government echoed this sentiment through the call to make Palestine a British governed mandate under the new League of Nations. This stance was only partly driven by imperial considerations. It was also the product of British support for the creation of a Jewish state in Palestine embodied in the Balfour Declaration.

This document, being the product of the force of Zionism, was a further destabilizing element to Allenby's efforts to keep stable the conquered territory under his command. Indeed, many writers after the war linked the Battle of Megiddo and the subsequent campaigns to a holy crusade that allowed for the establishment of a Jewish home state. Allenby outright rejected this notion in a 1933 speech to a chapter of the YMCA:

---

35 A.J.P. Taylor, ed., *Lloyd George: A Diary by Frances Stevenson* (New York: Harper and Row, 1971), 174.
36 Lloyd George, 691-692.
37 Gurdun Krämer, *A History of Palestine: From the Ottoman Conquest to the Founding of the State of Israel*, Translated by Graham Harman and Gudrun Krämer (Princeton: Princeton University Press, 2008), 147-148.
38 Great Britain, National Archives, War Cabinet Records, Sykes to Hankey, 7 April 1917, CAB 21/96, 4.

Our campaign has been called the "Last Crusade." It was not a crusade. There is still a current idea that our object was to deliver Jerusalem from the Moslem. Not so. Many of my soldiers were Moslems. The importance of Jerusalem lay in its strategical [sic] position. There was no religious impulse in this campaign. The sole object of every man in my army was to win the war.[39]

This stance was certainly one that Allenby held during the war. He saw himself as a military leader rather than a political creature on a romantic crusade. He also stood against this romantic notion due to the fact that Zionism threatened the stability of Palestine in trying to create a Jewish home state in a region whose population was predominately Arab Muslims. In March 1919 the authorities administering Palestine under Allenby estimated that the population of Palestine was 648,000 people. Of these 551,000 were Muslim, 65,300 were Jewish, 62,500 were Christians, and 5,050 people counted themselves as member of other faiths.[40] Given these numbers he felt that the possibility of implementing the Zionist vision for Palestine would lead to massive unrest. As a result when Allenby had conquered all of Palestine he pursued the same policy as that towards Syria. He forbade any Zionist activity that might provoke the Arabs of the region. He also banned the singing of the Zionist national anthem *Hatikvah* as well as the use of Zionist symbols and the Zionist national flag. In terms of the latter, Allenby specifically mandated that only the Union Jack would be flown in Palestine.

Notwithstanding his attitude, Allenby was forced to deal with Zionism in Palestine because of the support of the movement by Prime Minister Lloyd George's government. Not only had the British committed to the creation of the Jewish state through the Balfour Declaration, but Dr. Chaim Weizmann, being the chief proponent of Zionism during the war, held the favor of Lloyd George. Zionist activity in Palestine as a consequence created an atmosphere that greatly concerned Allenby as he saw the implementation of the Balfour Plan as unworkable. On 16 August 1919, Allenby wrote that "In Palestine the anti-Jewish feeling is now very acute. Muslims and Christians are united in their opposition to the Jews."[41] While the question of British control over Palestine was settled at the April 1920 San Remo Conference that made the territory a League of Nations mandate under the British, the problem of instability over the implementation of the Balfour Declaration remained and deepened.

The San Remo Conference was the culmination of diplomatic efforts at the Paris Peace Conference to decide the fate of all territory captured by Allenby's troops. This

---

39   Great Britain, Liddell Hart Centre for Military Archives, King's College, London, The Papers of Sir Edmund Allenby, "Notes from a lecture given by Allenby at YMCA", 6/VIII/70.
40   Krämer, 156.
41   Allenby to Reginald Wingate, 16 August 1919, in Matthew Hughes, ed., *Allenby in Palestine: The Middle East Correspondence of Field Marshal Viscount Allenby, June 1917–October 1919*, 285.

process began in earnest with the creation in June 1919 of the King-Crane Commission whose task was to determine the wishes of the inhabitants in Palestine and Syria concerning their political future. The publication of the commission's report at the end of July did nothing to settle the fate of the region. The report concluded that there was overwhelming hostility to the presence of the French in Syria, which led to the French rejecting the commission altogether. Not only did this leave the future of the region undecided, but it also emboldened Emir Feisal in his efforts to create an Arab state in Syria. Feisal's machinations only further deepened the problems associated with Allenby's efforts to maintain control of his captured territory. Compounding the situation was also the fact that the Egyptian Expeditionary Force by June 1919 was being demobilized, which threatened the ability of the British to maintain any control in what was a political power vacuum.

Ultimately, it was the demobilization of the Egyptian Expeditionary Force that necessitated a conclusion to the acrimonious debate over who would command the Near Middle East. The French, despite the protests of Feisal, were recognized by the British as the future mandatory power of Syria as well as modern day Lebanon. In essence, Lloyd George had felt compelled to stand by the French given the original Sykes-Picot Agreement and the decreasing power of the British in the region through demobilization. As a result, the British set 1 November 1919 as the date for their withdrawal from Syria with French troops replacing them as part of the construction of the French mandate. Allenby's reaction was one where he believed there would be bloodshed between the French and Arabs on the withdrawal of British troops. Even so, Allenby went forward with plans to evacuate the territory that his soldiers had fought to conquer.[42] On 25 July 1920 French troops moved into Damascus in a world where the San Remo Conference had officially recognized France as the mandatory power of both Syria and modern day Lebanon. The Arabs under Emir Feisal could do little to alter this outcome in the face of having both no support from their former British allies and being rejected by the other great powers in their call for their own nationalist state. The French occupation of Syria and Lebanon was the culminating event that reshaped the entire Middle East. This redefinition was precipitated by the Battle of Megiddo.

Indeed Allenby's triumph serves as a shining example of how the world was never the same after the 1918 Armistice. Ottoman rule in the Middle East was replaced by a series of artificial states governed by European imperial masters. Although today the Europeans are no longer in power in the region, the Middle East still lives with the consequences of Megiddo through instability within these artificial constructs and through the creation of Israel. The Battle of Megiddo, while being one of the greatest military triumphs of the First World War, carried with it enormous political ramifications that continue to reverberate throughout an unstable Middle East. The battle serves as only one example of the fact that today's world lives with the consequences of a war that began over a century ago.

---

42 Great Britain, National Archives, "The Evacuation of Syria", 10 October 1919, WO 32/5730.

Bibliography

Archival Sources

Australian War Memorial
  AWM 4: First Australian Imperial Force War Diary
Great Britain, Imperial War Museum, Department of Documents
  Alan-Williams, A.C.
  Argyle, E.P.
  Baily, V.H.
  Chetwode, Philip
  Hampton, Lord
  Lambert, A.F.
  Mead, W.G.
  O'Sullivan, J.F.B.
  Powell, E.S.
  Routhon, N.F.
  Wilson, R.H.
Great Britain, National Archives
  CAB 21, CAB 38: Memoranda of the Committee of Imperial Defense
  CAB 23/6, CAB 23/7: War Cabinet Secretariat Papers
  CAB 24: Minutes of the War Cabinet
  CAB 42: War Council Papers
  FO 371: Foreign Office, General Correspondence
  FO 800: Papers of Lord Curzon
  FO 882: Papers of the Arab Bureau
  WO 95: Unit War Diaries of the British Army
  WO 106: Directorate of Military Operations and Intelligence
Liddell Hart Centre for Military Archives, King's College, London
  GB0099 KCLMA Allenby: Papers of General Edmund Allenby
  GB0099 KCLMA Bartholomew: Papers of Sir William Henry Bartholomew
  GB 0099 KCLMA Shea: Papers of Sir John Stuart Mackenzie Shea

Published Sources

Al-Askari, Jafar Pasha. *A Soldier's Story: From Ottoman Rule to Independent Iraq.* London: Arabian Publishing, 2003.
Barrow, George de S. *The Fire of Life.* London: Hutchinson, 1942.
Barrow, George de S. *Two Cavalry Episodes in the Palestine Campaign of 1917-1918.* London: J.J. Keliher, 1919.
Bourne, Kenneth and D. Cameron Watt, eds. *British Documents on Foreign Affairs: Reports and Papers from the Foreign Office Confidential Print.* Part II. *From the First o the Second World War.* Series I. *The Paris Peace Conference of 1919.* Dockrill, M. ed. Volume 1. *Preparations for the Conference and Early Meetings.* Frederick, MD: University Publications of America, 1991.
———. *British Documents on Foreign Affairs: Reports and Papers from the Foreign Office Confidential Print.* Part II. *From the First to the Second World War.* Series I. *The Paris Peace Conference of 1919.* Dockrill, M. ed. Volume 2. *Supreme Council Minutes, January-March 1919.* Frederick, MD: University Publications of America, 1991.
———. *British Documents on Foreign Affairs: Reports and Papers from the Foreign Office Confidential Print.* Part II. *From the First to the Second World War.* Series I. *The Paris Peace Conference of 1919.* Dockrill, M. ed. Volume 3. *Supreme Council Minutes, March-July 1919; British Empire Delegation Minutes, January-March 1919.* Frederick, MD: University Publications of America, 1989.
———. *British Documents on Foreign Affairs: Reports and Papers from the Foreign Office Confidential Print.* Part II. *From the First to the Second World War.* Series I. *The Paris Peace Conference of 1919.* Dockrill, M. ed. Volume 4. *British Empire Delegation Minutes, March-June 1919; Reports of Paris Peace Conference Commissions.* Frederick, MD: University Publications of America, 1989.
———. *British Documents on Foreign Affairs: Reports and Papers from the Foreign Office Confidential Print.* Part II. *From the First to the Second World War.* Series I. *The Paris Peace Conference of 1919.* Dockrill, M. ed. Volume 11. *The Turkish Settlement and the Middle East; the Far East.* Frederick, MD: University Publications of America, 1991.
———. *British Documents on Foreign Affairs: Reports and Papers from the Foreign Office Confidential Print.* Part II. *From the First to the Second World War.* Series B. *Turkey, Iran, and the Middle East, 1918-1939.* Bidwell, Robin, ed. Volume 1. *The End of the War, 1918-1920.* Frederick, MD: University Publications of America, 1985.
Curry, Sister Ethel. "A Prisoner in Aleppo," *Nurses' League Journal,* VII, Kensington, London: December 1919.
Dalbiac, P.H. *History of the 60th Division.* London: George Allen and Unwin, 1927.
Djemal Pasha. *Memories of a Turkish Statesman: 1913-1919.* New York: George H. Doran, 1922.
Ege, Ragip Nurettin. Gunes N. Ege-Akter, trans. *By the Light of the Candle: The Diaries of a Reserve Officer in the Ottoman Army.* Istanbul: Dergah Yayinlari, 2006.
Garnett, David, ed. *The Letters of T.E. Lawrence.* New York: Doubleday, 1939.

Gibbons, T. *With the 1/5th Essex in the East*. Colchester, UK: Benham, 1921.
Gilbert, Vivian. *The Romance of the Last Crusade: With Allenby to Jerusalem*. New York: D. Appleton, 1923.
Goodsall, Robert H. *Palestine Memories*. Canterbury, UK: Cross and Jackman, 1925.
Gordon, H. Pirie. *A Brief Record of the Advance of the Egyptian Expeditionary Force*. London, HMSO: 1919.
Great Britain, *The Official History of the War: Military Operations, Egypt and Palestine. Maps*. London: HMSO, 1930.
Great Britain, British Library, Oriental and India Office Collections, "Nominal Rolls of Indian Prisoners of War, Suspected of Having Derted to the Enemy or of Having Given Information to or Otherwise Assisted the Enemy After Capture: Egyptian Expeditionary Force," L/MIL/17/5/2403.
Hughes, Matthew, ed. *Allenby in Palestine: The Middle East Correspondence of Field Marshal Viscount Allenby, June 1917-October 1919*. Stroud: Sutton Publishing, 2004.
Jeffrey, Keith, ed. *The Military Correspondence of Field Marshal Sir Henry Wilson, 1918-1922*. London: Army Records Society, 1985.
Lloyd George, David. *Memoirs of the Paris Peace Conference*. Volume II. New Haven: Yale University Press, 1939.
———. *War Memoirs of David Lloyd George*. Volume 6. *1918*. Boston: Little, Brown, 1937.
Meinertzhagen, Richard. *Middle East Diary, 1917-1956*. New York: Thomas Yoseloff, 1960.
Montagu, Edwin. *An Indian Diary*. London: William Heinemann, 1930.
Morgenthau, Henry. *Ambassador Morgenthau's Story*. New York: Doubleday, 1918.
Murphy, C.C.R. *The History of the Suffolk Regiment, 1914-1927*. London: Hutchinson and Patterson, 1928.
Sanders, Liman. *Five Years in Turkey*. Annapolis: Naval Institute Press, 1927.
Taylor, A.J.P., ed. *Lloyd George: A Diary by Frances Stevenson*. New York: Harper and Row, 1971.
Teichman, O. *The Diary of a Yeomanry M.O.* . London: T. Fisher and Unwin, 1921.
Woodward, David, ed. *The Military Correspondence of Field Marshal William Robertson, Chief of the Imperial General Staff, December 1915-February 1918*. London: Army Records Society, 1989.
Woodward, E.L. and Butler, Rohan, eds. *Documents on British Foreign Policy, 1919-1939*. First Series. Volume 4. London: HMSO, 1952.

Published Secondary Sources

Anglesey, George Charles. *A History of the British Cavalry, 1816-1919*. Volume 5. *Egypt, Palestine, and Syria, 1914-1919*. London: Leo Cooper, 1994.

Badcock, G.E. *A History of the Transport Services of the Egyptian Expeditionary Force, 1916-1917-1918*. London: Hugh Rees, 1925.

Barr, James. *A Line in the Sand: The Anglo-French Struggle for the Middle East, 1914-1948*. New York: Norton, 2012.

Barua, Pradeep P. *Gentlemen of the Raj: The Indian Army Officer Corps, 1817-1949*. Westport, Conn.: Praeger, 2003.

Bell, Archibald, *A History of the Blockade of Germany and the Countries Associated with Her in the Great War: Austria-Hungary, Bulgaria, and Turkey, 1914-1918*. London: HMSO, 1961.

Biger, Gideon. *The Boundaries of Modern Palestine, 1840-1947*. London: Routledge, 2004.

Bruce, A.P.C. *The Last Crusade: The Palestine Campaign in the First World War*. London: John Murray, 2002.

Bullock, David. *Allenby's War: The Palestine-Arabian Campaigns, 1916-1918*. London: Blandford Press, 1988.

Busch, Briton Cooper. *Britain, India, and the Arabs, 194-1921*. Berkeley: University of California Press, 1971.

Butler, Daniel Allen. *In the Shadow of the Sultan's Realm: The Destruction of the Ottoman Empire and the Creation of the Modern Middle East*. Washington, DC: Potomac Books, 2011.

Chakravorty, Upendra Narayan. *Indian Nationalism and the First World War, 1914-1918: Recent Political and Economic History of India*. Calcutta: Progressive Publishers, 1997.

Cline, Eric. *The Battles of Armageddon: Megiddo and the Jezreel Valley from the Bronze Age to the Nuclear Age*. Ann Arbor, MI: University of Michigan Press, 2000.

Cutlack, F.M. *The Official History of Australia in the War of 1914-1918*. Volume 8. *The Australian Flying Corps in the Western and Eastern Theaters of War, 1914-1918*. Sydney, Australia: Angus and Robertson, 1923.

Darwin, J. *Britain, Egypt, and the Middle East: Imperial Policy in the Aftermath of the War, 1918-1922*. New York: St. Martin's Press, 1981.

Ellinwood, DeWitt C. and S.D. Pradhan, eds. *India and World War I*. Columbia, MO: South Asia Books, 1978.

Erickson, Edward. *Ordered to Die: A History of the Ottoman Army in the First World War*. Westport, Conn.: Greenwood Press, 2001.

———. *Ottoman Army Effectiveness in World War I: A Comparative Study*. New York: Routledge, 2007.

———. *Palestine: The Ottoman Campaigns of 1914-1918*. Havertown: Pen and Sword, 2016.

Falls, Cyril. *Armageddon, 1918*. London: Weidenfeld and Nicolson, 1964.

———. *History of the Great War, based on Official Documents, Military Operations Egypt and Palestine, 1914-1918*. Volume II. *From June 1917 to the End of the War.* London: HMSO, 1930.
Ford, Roger. *Eden to Armageddon: World War I in the Middle East.* New York: Pegasus Books, 2010.
Friedman, Isaiah. *British Pan-Arab Policy, 1915-1922: A Critical Appraisal.* London: Transaction Publishers, 2010.
———. *The Question of Palestine, 1914-1918: British-Jewish-Arab Relations.* New York: Schocken Books, 1973.
Gardner, Brian. *Allenby of Arabia: Lawrence's General.* New York: Coward-McCann, 1965.
Garsia, Clive. *A Key to Victory: A Study in War Planning.* London: Eyre and Spottiswoode, 1940.
Grainger, John. *The Battle for Palestine, 1917.* Woodbridge, Suffolk, UK: Boydell Press, 2006.
———. *The Battle for Syria, 1918-1920.* Woodbridge: Boydell and Breyer, 2013.
Gilmour, David. *Curzon: Imperial Statesman.* New York: Farrar, Straus, and Giroux, 1994.
Grey, Jeffrey. *A Military History of Australia.* New York: Cambridge University Press, 1999.
Gullet, H.S. *The Official History of Australia in the War of 1914-1918*, Vol. 7, *Sinai and Palestine: The Australian Imperial Force in Sinai and Palestine, 1914-1918.* Sydney: Angus and Robertson, 1923.
Hamilton, Richard F. and Holger H. Herwig. *Decisions for War, 1914-1917.* Cambridge: Cambridge University Press, 2004.
Hankey, Maurice. *The Supreme Command, 1914-1918.* London: George Allen and Unwin, 1961.
Higham, Robin and Dennis Showalter. *Researching World War I: A Handbook.* Westport, Conn.: Greenwood Press, 2003.
Hill, Alec. *Chauvel of the Light Horse: A Biography of General Sir Harry Chauvel.* Melbourne, Australia: Melbourne University Press, 1978.
Hughes, Matthew. *Allenby and British Strategy in the Middle East, 1917-1919.* London: Frank Cass, 1999.
James, Lawrence, *Imperial Warrior: The Life and Times of Field-Marshal Viscount Allenby, 1861-1936.* London: Weidenfeld and Nicolson, 1993.
James, Lawrence. *Raj: The Making and Unmaking of British India.* New York: St. Martin's Press, 1998.
Kent, Marian, ed. *The Great Powers and the End of the Ottoman Empire.* London: George Allen and Unwin, 1984.
Kinross, Lord. *Ataturk: A Biography of Mustapha Kemal, Father of Modern Turkey.* New York: William Morrow and Company, 1965.
Kiracofe, Clifford. *Dark Crusade: Christian Zionism and US Foreign Policy.* London: I.B. Taurus, 2009.

Krämer, Gudrun. *A History of Palestine: From the Ottoman Conquest to the Founding of the State of Israel*. Translated by Graham Harman and Gudrun Kramer. Princeton: Princeton University Press, 2008.

Kushner, David, ed. *Palestine in the the Late Ottoman Period: Political, Social, and Economic Transformation*. Leiden, Netherlands: E.J. Brill, 1986.

Levey, Zach and Elie Podesh, eds. *Britain and the Middle East: From Imperial Power to Junior Partner*. Brighton, UK: Sussex Academy Press, 2008.

Mansfield, Peter. *A History of the Middle East*. New York: Viking, 1991.

Maxwell, Donald. *The Last Crusade*. London: John Lane, 1920.

McDowall, R.J.S. "The Water Supply of the Egyptian Expeditionary Force, with Special Reference to the Efficeincy of Mechanical Rapid Filtration with Chlorination," *The Journal of Hygiene*, January 1921, Volume 19, Number 3, pp. 305-308.

Morrow, John. *The Great War: An Imperial History*. New York: Routledge, 2004.

Mortlock, Michael J. *The Egyptian Expeditionary Force in World War I: A History of the British-Led Campaigns in Egypt, Palestine, and Syria*. Jefferson, North Carolina: McFarland, 2011.

Muhammad, Shan. *The Indian Muslims: A Documentary History*. Meenakshi, Prakashan, India, 1982.

Nevakivi, Jukka. *Britain, France, and the Middle East, 1914-1920*. London: Athlone Press, 1969.

Newell, Jonathan. "Allenby and the Palestine Campaign" in Brian Bond, ed., *The First World War and British Military History*, 188-226. Oxford: Clarendon Press, 1991.

Oliver-Dee, Sean. *The Caliphate Question: The British Government and Islamic Governance*. New York: Lexington Books, 2009.

Omissi, David, ed. *Indian Voices of the Great War, 1914-1918*. New York: St. Martin's Press, 1999.

Osborne, Eric W. *Britain's Economic Blockade of Germany, 1914-1919*. London: Frank Cass, 2004.

Özdemir, Hikmet. *The Ottoman Army, 1914-1918: Disease and Death on the Battlefield*. Salt Lake City, University of Utah Press, 2008.

Pappé, Ilan. *A History of Modern Palestine: One Land, Two Peoples*. Cambridge: Cambridge University Press, 2004.

Perrett, Bryan. *Megiddo 1918: Lawrence, Allenby, and the March on Damascus*. Westport, Conn.: Praeger, 2004.

Povlock, Paul. *Deep Battle in World War I: The British 1918 Offensive in Palestine*. San Francisco: Verdun Press, 1997.

Prasad, Yuvaraj Deva. *The Indian Muslims and World War I: A Phase of Disillusionment with British Rule, 1914-1918*. New Delhi: Janaki Prakashan, 1985. Press Publishing, *The World Almanac and Encyclopedia, 1914*. New York: Press Publishing, 1913.

Preston, R.M.P. *The Desert Mounted Corps: An Account of the Cavalry Operations in Palestine and Syria, 1917-1918*. New York: Houghton Mifflin, 1923.

Raleigh, Walter Alexander. *The War In the Air: Being the Story of the Part Played in the Great War by the Royal Air Force*. Volume 6. Oxford: Clarendon Press, 1937.

Roy, Kaushik, ed. *The Indian Army in the Two World Wars*. Boston: Brill, 2012.

Savage, Raymond. *Allenby of Armageddon: The Career and Campaigns of Field Marshal Viscount Allenby*. Indianapolis: Bobbs-Merrill, 1926.

Shaw, Stanford J. *The Ottoman Empire in World War I*. Volume 1. *Prelude to War*. Ankara: Turkish Historical Society, 2006.

———. *The Ottoman Empire in World War I*. Volume 2. *Triumph and Tragedy, November 1914-July 1916*. Ankara: Turkish Historical Society, 2008.

Sheffy, Yigal. "British Intelligence in the Middle East, 1900-1918: How Much Do We Know?," *Intelligence and National Security*, Spring 2002, Vol. 17, Issue 1, pp. 33-52.

———. *British Military Intelligence in the Palestine Campaign, 1914-1918*. London: Frank Cass, 1998.

———. "Chemical Warfare and the Palestine Campaign, 1916-1918," *The Journal of Military History*, July 2009, Volume 73, Number 3, pp. 803-844.

Shorrock, W.I. *French Imperialism in the Middle East: The Failure of Policy in Syria and Lebanon, 1900-1914*. Madison, WI: University of Wisconsin Press, 1976.

Smith, George. *The Historical Geography of the Holy Land*. London: Hodder and Stoughton, 1908.

Steuber, Werner. *Jildirim: Deutsche Streiter auf heiligem Boden*. Oldenburg, Stalling, 1924.

Sumida, Jon. *In Defense of Naval Supremecy: Finance, Technology, and British Naval Policy 1889-1914*. Boston, MA: Unwin Hyman, 1989.

Tamari, Salim. *Year of the Locust: A Soldier's Diary and the Erasure of Palestine's Ottoman Past*. Berkeley: University of California Press, 2011.

Thorau, Peter. *Lawrence von Arabien: Ein Mann und seine Zeit*. Munchen: Verlag C.H. Beck, 2010.

Tucker, Spencer C. ed. *The Encyclopedia of World War I: A Political, Social, and Military History*. 5 Volumes. Santa Barbara, CA.: ABC-CLIO, 2005.

Ulrichsen, Kristian Coates. *The Logistics and Politics of the British Campaigns in the Middle East, 1914-1922*. New York: Palgrave, Macmillan, 2011.

Van der Kloot, William. *The Lessons of War: The Expeiences of Seven Future Leaders in the First World War*. The Mill, Brinscombe Port, Stroud, Gloucestershire, United Kingdom: History Press, 2008.

Van der Vat, Dan. *The Ship that Changed the World: The Escape of the Goeben to the Dardenelles in 1914*. Bethesda, MD: Adler and Adler, 1986.

Verma, D.C. *Indian Armed Forces in Egypt and Palestine, 1914-1918*. New Delhi: Rajesh, 2004.

Wavell, Archibald. *Allenby: A Study in Greatness*. New York: Oxford University Press, 1941.

———. *The Palestine Campaigns*. London: Constable, 1941.

Westrate, Bruce. *The Arab Bureau: British Policy in the Middle East, 1916-1920*. University Park, PA.: Pennsylvania State University Press, 1992.

Woodward, David R. *Hell in the Holy Land: World War I in the Middle East.* Lexington, KY: University Press of Kentucky, 2006.

———. *Field Marshal Sir William Robertson: Chief of the Imperial General Staff in the Great War.* Westport, Conn.: Praeger, 1998.

Zisser, Eyal. "Britain and the Levant, 1918-1946: A Missed Opportunity?" in *Britain and the Middle East: From Imperial Power to Junior Partner,* Zach Levy and Elie Podeh, eds., 133-152. Portland, Oregon: Sussex Academic Press, 2008.

Index

Aleppo, 21–23, 27, 32–33, 35, 46, 92–93, 95, 98–99, 101–2, 105
Allenby, General Sir Edmund, 34, 36, 39, 40, 42–51, 57–61, 68–69, 72, 74–75, 77, 90–99, 101–8, 111, 113–15
Amman, 47, 62, 87–88, 103
Aqaba, 15–16, 31, 36
Arabs, 31–32, 34, 88, 94–97, 103–8, 112

Baghdad Railroad, 13–14, 21
Balfour Declaration (1917), 106–7
Barrow, Major-General Sir G. de S, 49, 72–73, 79–80, 87, 93–94, 110
Beersheba, 22, 28–29, 36, 39–41, 43, 45, 59
Beirut, 18, 23, 37, 98, 104
Beisan, 58, 60, 72, 79–81, 86, 92–93, 95
Bulfin, Lieutenant General Sir Edward, 64, 68–69, 78, 93

Cars, armoured, 79–80
Caucasia, 25–26
Central Powers, 19–20, 35, 37–38, 45–46
Chauvel, Major General Sir Henry 64, 73, 82, 90, 92, 95–97
Chaytor, Major General Edward, 62, 65, 75, 86–89
Chetwode, Lieutenant General Sir Philip, 65, 74, 79, 84, 93, 109
Committee of Imperial Defense, 14, 16–18

Damascus, 28, 31–33, 85, 87, 91, 93–98, 100, 102–3, 105, 108, 114
Dardanelles, 20, 29–30

Davison, Captain D.S., 73, 79–80

Egypt, 12, 15–17, 19, 21, 26–29, 31–53, 59, 88, 94

Feisal, Emir, 58, 96–98, 104–5, 108
Formations:
British, Empire & Commonwealth
    Egyptian Expeditionary Force (EEF), 23, 34–36, 39–43, 45–46, 48–49, 51–53, 55–60, 62–63, 68, 74–75, 83–87, 89, 91–92, 94–95, 101–2, 105–6, 108
    Australian Imperial Force (AIF), 62, 74, 92, 113
    Australian Light Horse, 82, 92
    Camel Transport Corps, 39
    Desert Mounted Corps, 49, 51, 58–59, 61–62, 64, 66, 68–69, 72, 74, 77–80, 82, 85, 89, 95–96, 99–100
    Lahore Division, 64, 77, 83
    Meerut Division, 70–71
    New Zealand Mounted Division, 51, 65
    54th East Anglian Division, 65, 71
Ottoman/German
    Fourth Army, 75, 86–89, 93–94, 99
    Seventh Army, 55-56, 63–64, 66, 74, 78–79, 84-87
    Eighth Army, 57, 63-64, 66, 68–69, 76–77, 84-87, 90, 99
    II Corps, 64, 88, 94
    III Corps, 64
    XXII Corps, 64, 77
    Asia Korps, 44, 61, 64, 74, 76–78, 86, 90, 100

Gaza, 22, 26, 29, 41-45

Haidar Pasha, 21–23, 63
Haifa, 17–18, 89–90, 102, 106
Hussein, King, 32–33

Istanbul, 14, 16, 19–26, 28, 31–32, 56, 63, 100, 102

Jaffa, 22, 36–37, 46, 53, 62, 68
Jenin, 66, 77, 82–83, 92–93
Jericho, 36, 47, 75, 87
Jerusalem, vi, 36, 41, 45–47, 50, 53, 56, 59, 61, 103, 107
Jordan valley, 36, 58, 61–62, 64–65, 74–75, 79, 83, 86–87

Kantara, 16, 40
Kemal, Mustapha, 55, 63, 74, 79, 100–101,
Kitchener, Field Marshal Lord Herbert, 32
Kressenstein, General Kress von, 28, 45

Lake Tiberias, 36, 63
Lawrence, T.E., 18–19, 44, 62, 85, 93–94, 97
Lloyd George, David, 11, 37, 39, 42, 46, 104–5

Maunsell, Lieutenant Colonel Francis, 18–19
Maxwell, General Sir John, 29–30, 114
Mesopotamia, 11–12, 15, 21, 25–27, 30–33, 38, 42, 44, 49, 106
Mount Carmel, 89–90
Murray, General Sir Archibald, 35, 37, 39–43, 55

Nablus, 57–58, 64, 66, 69, 79, 84, 86, 103
Nazareth, 18, 58, 64, 72–73, 80–82, 86
Northern Palestine, 36, 60

Ottoman Empire, v–vi, 11–27, 30–34, 42, 55, 63, 91, 112–13

Paris Peace Conference (1919), 3, 105, 107
Persian Gulf, 15–16, 33
Plain of Esdraelon, 36, 58, 69, 72–73, 79–80, 87

Raffa, 15, 39
Rayak, 21–22, 100
Robertson, General Sir William, 35, 37-39, 41, 45, 47, 45–48, 62, 75, 83, 92
Royal Air Force (RAF), 51, 60–61, 66, 75, 82, 84–86

Samakh, 86, 90–91
Sanders, General Liman von, 24–25, 55, 61, 63–64, 66, 72, 77, 81–82, 91, 100
Suez Canal, 12, 16–18, 21, 26–30, 34–35, 37, 39, 41, 44
Supreme War Council, 47
Sykes-Picot Agreement (1916), 33–34, 96–98, 103–4, 106, 108
Syria, 15, 17–22, 26–28, 30, 32–37, 39–40, 44, 55–56, 87–88, 91–92, 97–100, 102–8

Thrace, 21, 25–26, 100
Tul Karm, 64, 66, 68–69, 77–78

Wahaby, General Ali Bey, 88–89
War Cabinet, 38, 42, 45–46, 48, 96, 104
War Office, 18–19, 48, 50, 103
Western Front, 21, 27, 30, 35, 37–38, 41, 43, 45–50, 101

Young Turks, 19, 28

Zionism, 30, 52, 106–7